F2

CHINA PAINTING

To my family for their cooperation; to my teacher, Aure D. Payne who shared her skill; to my students for their help in making this book possible.

CHINA PAINTING

STEP BY STEP

DORIS W. TAYLOR
ANNE BUTTON HART

Photographs by DARLENE BEKKHEDAL

VNR VAN NOSTRAND REINHOLD COMPANY
NEW YORK   CINCINNATI   TORONTO   LONDON   MELBOURNE

VAN NOSTRAND REINHOLD COMPANY Regional Offices:
New York Cincinnati Chicago Millbrae Dallas

VAN NOSTRAND REINHOLD COMPANY International Offices:
London Toronto Melbourne

Copyright © 1962 by LITTON EDUCATIONAL PUBLISHING, INC.
Library of Congress Catalog Card Number: 68-20912
ISBN 0-442-28441-1

Published by VAN NOSTRAND REINHOLD COMPANY
450 West 33rd Street, New York, N.Y. 10001

16 15 14 13 12 11 10 9 8 7 6 5 4 3 2 1

Foreword

This book is your passport to the fascinating and ancient art of china painting. Either as a hobby or for profit, china painting makes an interesting and absorbing pursuit.

Even if you think you have no artistic talents, you will find that by practicing diligently and studying the basic methods described in this book, china painting can become your talent.

For the first time, complete brush strokes—which are the clue to good painting—are illustrated in detail, and full instructions in step-by-step form are given for sixteen designs.

The text is profusely illustrated with more than ninety pages of line and wash drawings, and the three successive coats of paint applied to the china are clearly shown in the color plates. Painting on china has a delicate, translucent effect which differs from any other type of painting. Lighter colors applied in the first coat of paint show up through the darker colors which are applied successively.

In spite of the fact that china painting is centuries old as an art, all of the answers are still not known. We hope that you, as either beginners or advanced students, will use this book to improvise on your own, increasing your enjoyment as well as your skill. Remember that many professional studios have had small beginnings.

Doris Taylor
Alexandria, Virginia *June, 1962* Anne Button Hart
Falls Church, Virginia

Table of Contents

List of Illustrations

1

General Procedure

Unless you are doing monochrome painting or you are adding extra coats of paint purely to get more depth, the general procedure in all china painting is the same. Beginners in china painting should study the following steps before they begin so they can have an understanding of the basic method.

Choosing the China Piece

For practicing purposes or in doing a new design for the first time, select any flat piece. It will be easier to handle.

Be sure to match the quality of your piece to the amount of effort required to paint it. Reserve your maximum efforts for the best quality of china. The painting of dinnerware, for example, requires many hours, and so top grade china should be used.

NOTE: To aid in the reproduction of the color plates in this book, all paints were shaded darker than normal. Therefore, the finished china, painted as directed in the text, will appear lighter in color than in the color plate. In this book, the paintings have been made with china paints on paper. A special oil was concocted for the purpose so that the detail of the brush strokes could be clearly shown. The paintings indicate how the finished pieces will look. The drawings are shown in the actual size for finished pieces.

Designs

Trace the text design onto onionskin paper with a sharp pencil. Put a piece of wax graphite paper, used as transfer paper, on your china. Place the tracing over the graphite paper and hold firmly in position with clothespins or Scotch tape. You will have a better transfer if you sketch in the outlines rather than using a heavy solid line.

If you have traced the design with pencil, it is a good idea to use a colored pencil or a ball point pen over the black lines when transferring so as not to omit a part of the pattern accidentally.

As you acquire more assurance, you may sketch your drawings freehand with a china marker. Lines from your china marking pencil or your tracings will disappear in each firing process.

As a beginner or when doing a new trial design, mark over your wax lines with India ink, then wash off the wax lines with turpentine. If you make a painting mistake, you can wipe off the color with turpentine. The India ink line will still remain, but it will fire out. A heavy wax line will distort the color of the paint.

Commercial designs can be found at ceramic and hobby stores.

Preparation

Cover your work area with oilcloth or a plastic table cover. Cover yourself.

Beginners should study and memorize brush strokes (Chapter 4) before starting to paint.

Mixing Colors

Make sure your palette or tile is clean. Put a pea-sized amount of paint on the palette and a drop of medium. With the palette knife flat mix medium and paint until mixture has a consistency of thick paste. Use a circular motion while mixing. There should not be any loose, dry paint dust on the palette as it might blow into other colors and

2

distort them. Paint should be smooth without any grainy particles. Colors mixed with all-purpose medium (see page 9) will stay moist and usable for several days if covered with wax paper.

After you are more practiced, you may premix your colors with a special mixing medium which keeps them from drying out. There are many different commercial mixing mediums available, and you should test various types before you mix in quantity. There are two good ways to premix. You may premix on your working tile a double quantity of each color needed and then transfer it to the palette. For this purpose the palette should be divided into squares with India ink and each division marked with the name of the color it is to contain. Keep the palette covered and transfer only the colors you are using back to your working tile. The colors will remain moist or "open" for several weeks.

Another method of premixing is to mix a full vial of each color with mixing medium and store in a small jar with a tight cover. Use from this quantity as needed. Colors mixed in this manner should be mixed thicker than for painting. Thin the small quantity you are using with all-purpose medium before you start to paint.

Never dip the brush into *mixing* medium or use it to paint with. Its purpose is merely to keep paint open. Painting done with a mixing medium only will never dry. When painting, dip the brush into all-purpose medium.

Brush Conditioning

Clean the brush thoroughly in gum turpentine and wipe well before starting to paint. Condition the brush with medium and wipe (see Chapter 4).

With the brush flat and well spread, dip the tip into medium and wipe on the side of the jar. Using a C stroke, shade the paint on the brush so that the paint on the left side of the brush is heavy and on the right side it is light. You will have to stroke into the color eight or ten times in order to shade the brush properly. Rotate the china piece so that strokes are always made downward.

Between colors, wash the brush in turpentine and wipe it on a lint-free cloth. Dip the corner of the brush in oil, condition it, and proceed with a new color.

First Coat

The first coat of paint is very thin and is often referred to as a light wash. It is actually a flat, covering coat. It should be smooth and thin-looking on flowers and slightly heavier on leaves. If your brush does not give the desired results, do not patch. Wipe off what you have painted and repeat your stroke.

First background

Always use the same colors in backgrounding as are used in the main design, with the addition of pale yellow for sunshine effect. Keep background colors $1/4$ inch from the design. When you are padding over these colors (see Chapter 5), pad light colors first, changing the pad as you work into a new color. If you find you are removing too much of the design colors as you pad around it, *roll* the pad up to the design instead. If the oil creeps into the design, pad lightly or roll your finger over it to remove the excess.

Drying

Clean the bottom of the china with oil to remove smudges and finger marks. Do not use turpentine as this runs and can seep over the edge of the piece and spoil the painting on the front.

Label the piece with your name if desired, using a OO pointer or a quill pen. Any color on your palette may be thinned with a drop of anise oil to make a good writing fluid. Dry your piece overnight or for one hour in a slow oven.

If you are taking the piece out for commercial firing, wrap it carefully in wax paper or tissue paper.

4

First Firing

The first firing sets the design. After firing, the paint colors should be very pale and delicate looking. There should not be any ridged or raised paint. The surface of the piece should not be rough. All tracing lines will fire off in the kiln.

Second Coat

If you are a beginner, retrace your original design onto the china. This will help you in applying second coat.

When applying the second coat, it is essential that your brush be properly shaded with paint, for this coat of color is more difficult to apply than the first. Do not hesitate to wipe off and repeat if it is not satisfactory.

Second Background

A second background is optional. It adds depth to the colors but it tends to go on heavily. Use more oil and blend continuously with the brush. Roll your finger over the color to remove any excess. Take care to keep dark colors from overlapping onto the lighter first coat colors. Blend the edges.

Metallic trim

If you are a beginner, fire the second background before applying any metallic trim so as to prevent the oil from creeping over the trim. Any liquid trim must be aplied around a fired background only.

Second Firing

Third Coat

The third coat is the time for touching up and adding shadows. It also gives additional depth. Darkening adds depth, and contrast also adds depth.

Darken colors where flowers overlap and where leaves appear under flowers. Do not redo all the flowers and leaves. Add the second coat of metallic trim.

Third Firing

Erasing

Unfired paint can be removed while it is still wet with a lint-free cloth. If it has dried, coat your mistake with oil, let it sit for a few minutes and wipe off. If you have a major error it is usually better to clean off the piece entirely with gum turpentine and repeat the painting.

Firing will not correct painting mistakes. If any coat is not dark enough, you may reapply another coat with the same colors and fire again. Colors which have dried on your palette may be loosened with rectified oil of turpentine. Gum turpentine may be used but tends to make colors sticky.

2

Supplies

As a beginner in the field of china painting, you will probably prefer to make your first trial on a flat piece of china such as a plate or tile. Such pieces, known as white glazed vitreous china blanks, are readily available at your local ceramic stores and china painting studios. Most china shops carry one or two lines of pure white ware and will also order specially for customers. Qualities vary. Both German and Japanese china are common in the United States.

If you cannot find supplies in your area, look at the listings and advertisements in magazines such as *The China Decorator* (P.O. Box 36-C, Pasadena, California), *Popular Ceramics* (6061 Santa Monica Blvd., Los Angeles 38, Calif.), or *Ceramic Arts and Crafts* (Box 4011 Strathmoor Station, Detroit 27, Michigan). Many of the shops and studios mentioned in these monthly magazines sell china, china paints, designs and other equipment that you will need.

Beginners Check List of Materials

1. A covered china painter's palette is desirable but not essential. This is a glass slab and brush tray with a removable cover. A square white glazed tile or piece of heavy glass may be substituted for a palette. If you are using clear glass, be

7

sure to paste a piece of white paper on the underside to give you a background.

2. A palette knife for mixing paints.
3. Basic colors, as listed in Chapter 6.
4. Pen and several pen points, for signing names, dates, etc.
5. Outlining ink. This may also be made by adding a drop of anise oil to any mixed color.
6. A black wax china marking pencil.
7. India ink.
8. A gold eraser.
9. Graphite paper (must be wax graphite). If graphite is not available, a suitable substitute may be made by coating the back of onion skin tracing paper lightly with a black wax pencil.
10. Onionskin tracing paper.
11. Designs. You may trace designs directly from this book.
12. A bottle of all-purpose medium. A clean cold cream jar is good for holding medium.
13. Gum turpentine. A clean mustard jar is good for holding turpentine to clean brushes.
14. #4 and #8 square shader brushes; quill type.
15. OO pointer of sable or camel's hair.
16. ½-inch ferrule brush or #10 square shader for backgrounds.
17. Lamb's wool and pure silk cloths for making background pads.
18. A flat piece of glazed vitreous china.
19. Oilcloth to protect the work table.
20. A smock to protect clothes.
21. Nylon or other lint-free cloths for wiping brushes.
22. Anise oil for making ink; also for washing brushes before storing for any length of time.

As you advance in technique, you will want:

1. #1 through #12 square shaders; quill type.
2. ¾-inch ferrule brush or #12 square shader for doing backgrounds on large pieces.
3. Several #8 brushes to minimize washing.
4. A plate divider. This can be made by folding a large piece of paper into sections.
5. A sectional box (such as a fishing tackle box) for keeping supplies.
6. Small jars for premixing and storing paints.
7. Special mixing medium for premixing colors.
8. A grinding glass — optional but desirable for mixing large quantities of paint.
9. A covered palette — essential to the advanced painter as it helps to keep paints moist.
10. Additional colors. The colors you use the most may be purchased by the ounce, a more economical way.
11. Gold and separate gold tools. See Chapter 3 on gold for special instructions on this and other metallic finishes.
12. Special tinting medium to use in applying large backgrounds; it helps to keep paints in proper consistency.

Mediums

Advanced painters often prefer to mix their own mediums. Ingredients are available or can be ordered at drug stores. The basic formula for an all-purpose medium is:

32 parts balsam of Copaiba
1 part lavender oil
½ part clove oil

The final mixture should have the consistency of thin syrup. The balsam will vary in texture depending on its age. If your mixture is too thick, thin with clove oil, adding by the drop. If the mixture is too thin, add balsam.

A special tinting medium is desirable when painting large surfaces and backgrounding in order to keep paints workable for a longer period of time. The ratio should be:

2 tablespoons of regular mixing medium
3 drops of clove oil

Fat oil of turpentine may be used when necessary to dissolve gritty bits in the rose and ruby colors. Use a drop when mixing the dry color. (Fat oil of turpentine may be made by pouring 1/4 inch of turpentine into a saucer. Cover and let stand for several weeks, making sure to keep it free of dust.

Kiln

Ceramic stores do firing at reasonable costs. However, an 11-inch fire brick kiln is sufficient for most painters' need and requires no special wiring. See Chapter 23, on firing.

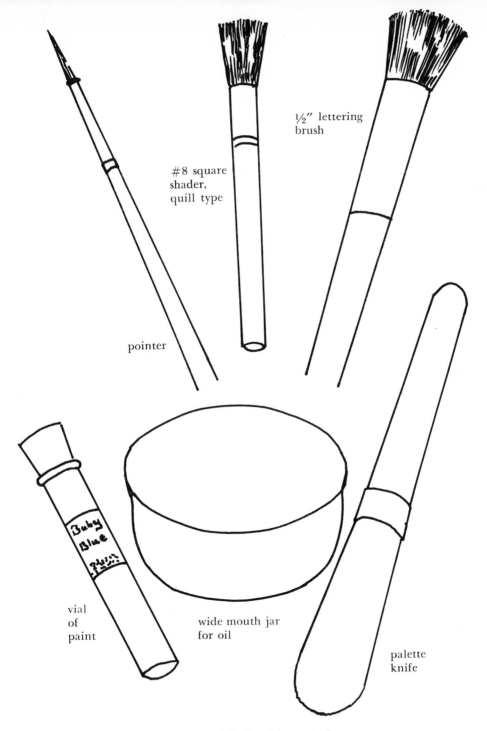

#8 square
shader,
quill type

½″ lettering
brush

pointer

Baby
Blue

vial
of
paint

wide mouth jar
for oil

palette
knife

Fig. 1. Materials for china painting

11

3

Gold and Other Metallic Finishes

All trimming supplies and tools must be kept separately and kept spotlessly clean. A separate palette knife and brush are necessary to be used exclusively for Roman gold work. There should be a separate brush for each liquid finish. To preserve cleanliness, wrap gold and equipment in wax paper when not in use. Before applying trimming, be sure your china surface is clean. Wipe the area carefully with a water-damp cloth. Where trim is to be applied, make sure all paint is removed from that area before firing.

Roman Gold

Roman gold, also known as burnish gold, can be purchased as a "pat" on a square of glass, or in paste form in a jar.

Roman gold has a rich, satin finish after final firing and polishing, although before the firing it is dark brown in color.

To mix the Roman gold, add a few drops of lavender oil to the pat and blend with a circular motion using your palette knife. Mixture should be sticky. It will run if the consistency is too thin.

Your brush should be dipped and cleaned in lavender oil along with your palette knife after every using. The same lavender oil may be used for both mixing and washing and the gold residue which will collect in the bottom of the bottle may be scooped out and reused. Always use a glass bottle for the oil, not a plastic one.

After firing, you can remove any smudges or marks with a gold eraser, which comes in stick or liquid form, or with a mild cleansing abrasive.

After final firing, Roman gold must be polished. There are several ways to polish gold. Dampen your fingertip in water, dip in English burnishing sand and rub lightly on the gold until it is shiny. Or, a glass polishing brush may be used. In this case, your fingers should be protected with gloves to prevent glass splinters. Small burnishing pads are also available.

There are two types of Roman gold, fluxed and unfluxed. Fluxed Roman gold is used on china for trimming. It cannot be applied over china color, fired or unfired. It is possible for fluxed Roman gold to be applied over a wax line without the wax impairing the gold. Sometimes it is advisable to trace in a pattern first before applying the gold. This is done with the wax pencil.

Unfluxed Roman gold is used on china for trimming over a fired color. If you gild over a fired china paint with a fluxed Roman gold, it will not adhere properly.

Two or three coats of gold are always necessary, firing between applications. If the gold does not appear solid after the second coat and firing, apply a third time and fire. If the gold has been applied too thickly, it will scale off after firing. Two or three thin applications are better than one thick one.

When applying gold rims, use your finger, rotating the plate as you work. In doing a design, use a square shader for coating large areas and a OO pointer for fine lines.

Stippling

A stippled gold edge is lovely. Cut off the hairs of an #8 brush halfway up, so that it is stubby (special stippling brushes can also be purchased). Dip the brush in paste Roman gold and dab around the edge of the plate. You may also use this process with any liquid finish. Pour a little in a flat dish and dip into the liquid with your brush. Separate brushes must be kept for each finish.

Liquid Gold

Liquid bright gold is a type of luster which is less expensive than the Roman gold and does not require burnishing but it gives a more metallic finish. It is a thin liquid, brown in color. It should flow easily from your brush and does not require thinning until it becomes old. In this event, thin with liquid gold essence until the proper consistency is obtained. Never mix liquid gold and turpentine, as this will cause the gold to turn purple.

Thin lines are easily made with liquid gold and this gold may be used as a first coat with the Roman gold applied over it. It will run into unfired colors so it should not be used near them. It cannot be used over wax lines.

Use liquid gold essence for thinning and washing your brush. Keep separate tools for liquid gold. For economy you may use liquid gold as a first coat and fluxed Roman gold as the second coat.

Silver Effects

White gold which comes in paste form gives an interesting effect. Although some varieties will tarnish eventually polishing will restore the appearance. Mix white gold with lavender oil. Liquid bright palladium also gives a silver effect and will not tarnish. Use palladium directly from the bottle.

Separate working tools are necessary with these finishes and liquid gold essence should be used to thin palladium, and to wash the brushes.

Palladium cannot be used over wax lines.

Do not apply any of these finishes over an unfired color.

Apply rims with the fingertip; use two thin coats as a general rule.

If after firing dull smudges appear, they can be removed with your gold eraser or a mild cleansing abrasive although this is difficult to do.

All liquid preparations should be fired at the same heat as your china paints (see Chapter 23).

A lovely effect can be achieved by using silver trim with black roses or with blue and gray monochrome designed dinnerware.

Platinum is applied and treated the same as palladium. It has the same fired effect but is usually more expensive.

Gold Outlining

Gold outlining is done with liquid gold, using either a OO pointer or a china pen. Simple outlining makes a china piece very attractive. Jewelry and accompanying sets of ring boxes, ring trees, and earring holders take gold outlining nicely and make unusual gifts, especially if they are personalized with names or dates. A desk set with the pen and pencil holders or a cigarette set with the box and lighter to match are also handsomely done with the gold outlining.

The china pen or OO pointer used for this process *must* be kept exclusively for gold outlining. Keep all utensils clean and free of dust. Before beginning to outline, wash the china piece in soap and water. Do *not* clean china with turpentine as it will distort the liquid gold.

Liquid gold cannot be applied over an unfired color nor can it be used over graphite or a china marking pencil. Therefore, the design should be applied freehand when liquid gold is to be used. Fire, apply the first coat of color and fire. Apply the second coat and fire.

If you must trace a design, you may trace it on first, then apply the first coat of color and fire. After firing do not retrace the design. Outline it with gold and fire. Apply the second coat of colors and fire.

4

Brush Technique

Good brush technique is essential to successful results in china painting. Shading the paint across the brush—heavy on the left end to light on the right end—is the most important step to master. As you learn to relax your hand and wrist you will find it easier to paint with the desired flowing motion.

Preparing the Brush

Immerse new brushes in all purpose medium before you use them. Wipe them well. Keep your brush flat and spread. Never allow it to come to a point. Flatten the brush hairs with your forefinger (Figure 2, top).

When preparing to use the brush, dip it in the medium, wipe it well and fan it out to double its original width. This is done by pressing it on the palette and pulling gently downward with a wavy motion (Figure 2, bottom). The correct brush to be used in painting a design is a brush which when spread is one half the width of the blossom or leaf.

Wash previously used brushes by swishing them back and forth in gum turpentine. Never use a stirring motion. Do not jab the brush on the bottom of the jar as this will break the bristles. If the brush

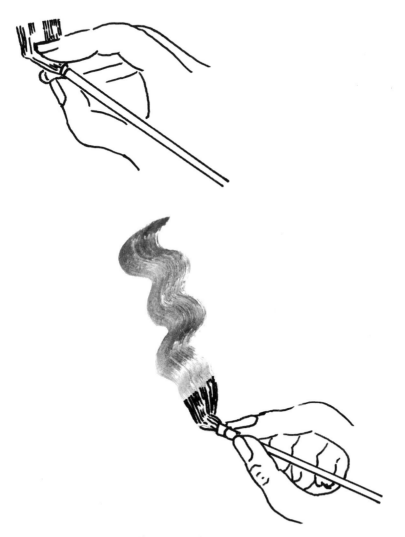

Fig. 2. Brush technique

is stiff, stand it in turpentine until it softens. Do not wipe the bottom of the turpentine jar with the brush. Wipe it well on a lint-free cloth before beginning to paint.

Loading the Brush

Dip the left corner of the brush into the oil, wipe it on the side of the jar and then load the brush by working it into the edge of paint with a circular C stroke motion, left side first. The brush should be touching the palette, and with each stroke it should pull a small portion of the paint out on the palette and across the brush. Ten or twelve strokes will be required to get the initial loading of paint on the brush.

Brush Strokes

Practice brush strokes first with the ½″ ferrule brush or the #10 square shader quill. As you progress to practicing with a #8 brush and then a #6 and #4 brush, you will find it difficult at first to shade and flatten the smaller brushes. Practice until you can do the strokes with all the brushes (Figure 3). All strokes should be made with a downward motion. When painting designs, continuously rotate the china so that each stroke is down.

When you have mastered and memorized the illustrated brush strokes with each size brush, practice tilting the brush and rolling the stem slightly between your fingers. In doing this, you will be starting the stroke with the left corner of the brush only. This gives a stroke which is narrow at the top, thicker in the middle and narrow at the base. Practice with each brush (Figure 4).

With the edge of a flattened brush, practice making a broken line and a feather stroke. A light stroke is used in painting stems, ferns, and pine needles. The harder you bear down on the brush, the wider the line. A heavier stroke is used in painting fern and buttercup leaves. Always stroke outward from the main design or

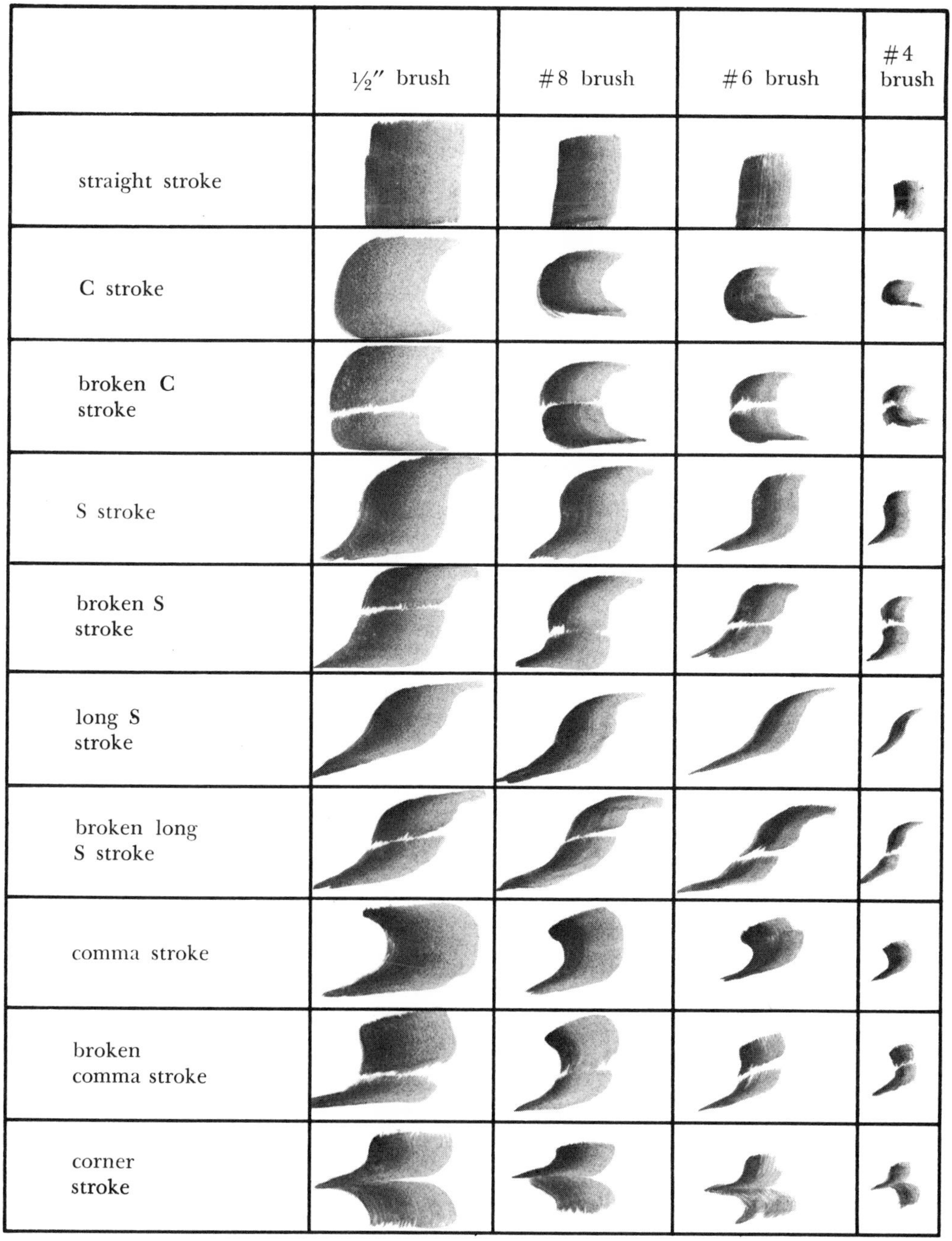

	½″ brush	#8 brush	#6 brush	#4 brush
straight stroke				
C stroke				
broken C stroke				
S stroke				
broken S stroke				
long S stroke				
broken long S stroke				
comma stroke				
broken comma stroke				
corner stroke				

Fig. 3. Brush strokes

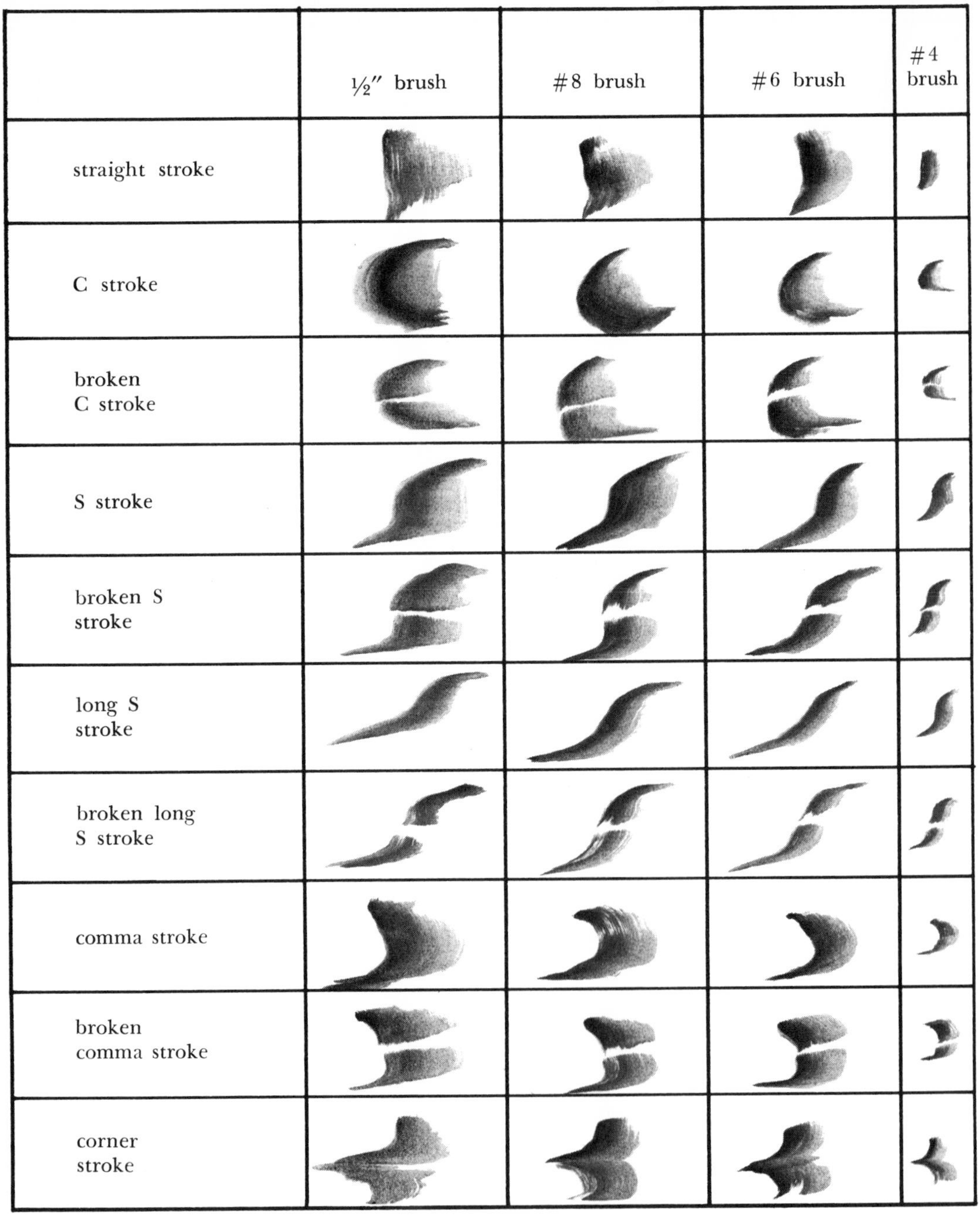

	½″ brush	#8 brush	#6 brush	#4 brush
straight stroke				
C stroke				
broken C stroke				
S stroke				
broken S stroke				
long S stroke				
broken long S stroke				
comma stroke				
broken comma stroke				
corner stroke				

Fig. 4. Brush strokes

20

branch when making stems or pine needles (Figure 5, top). Stroke in a curved downward motion when doing fern or leaves (Figure 5, bottom). Rotate the china as you work.

Care of the Brush

After using brushes, wash them well in turpentine, wipe them and flatten them between your thumb and forefinger. Store them in a jar with the brush side up or in a covered brush box. If the brush hairs are twisted, dip them in oil and stroke them on the palette with a wavy motion. Brushes which are to be stored for a long period should be washed in anise oil. *Never* wash brushes in soap and water. Ferrule brushes should never be allowed to sit in turpentine as it will loosen the brush hairs and they will fall out.

Fig. 5. Practice strokes

5

Backgrounds

Beginners

Backgrounding is one of the most important techniques in china painting. After you have mastered the brush strokes, you should practice backgrounding on a sample plate or tile which does not have a design. Figure 6 shows a beginner's technique.

Prepare pale yellow and baby blue paint but add one more drop of oil than you use when mixing regular paints. This will make the paint slightly thinner in consistency.

STEP 1 — Using a ½-inch brush, coat the plate with yellow.

STEP 2 — While the yellow is smooth but still moist, apply blue over the yellow.

STEP 3 — Wash the brush in turpentine, wipe, dip it into oil and wipe again. This gives a clean but oily brush. Dip the brush into the yellow and with a blending cross stroke join the two color lines.

STEP 4 — For padding, wrap a piece of lamb's wool in silk cloth. It should be the size of a small apple. Hold the ends in your palm making sure the pad is smooth and free of wrinkles. Pad the paint gently, first the yellow then the blue. This will give a delicate effect to the colors.

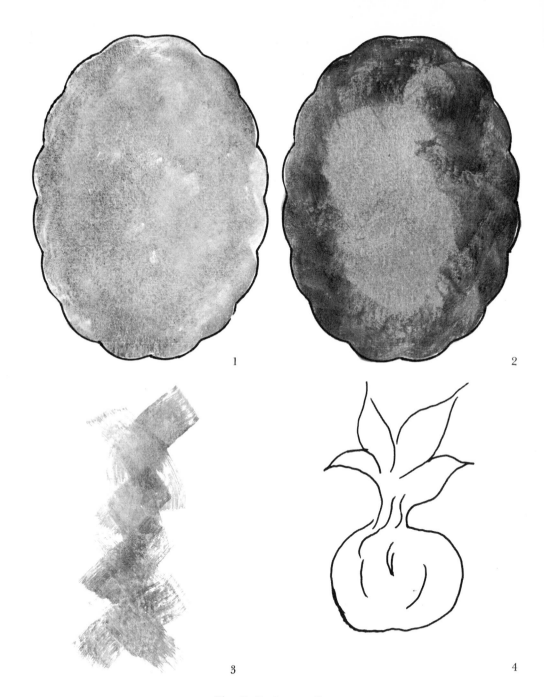

1

2

3

4

Fig. 6. Backgrounding

First Background

When you have become proficient enough to background around a design, proceed as described above, painting the background area up to a quarter-inch from the design. Wipe the brush completely dry (do not wash it in turpentine), then with the dry brush spread the background paint up to the design. Pad immediately, first the yellow, then the blue. Otherwise, the oil in the paint will seep over the design and distort it.

Pale backgrounds can only be obtained by applying the colors thinly and smoothly. A heavy background cannot be corrected after it has been fired. Remember that during the firing process the glaze on the china softens, but it can only absorb a thin coat of color.

You will want to use other colors in backgrounds besides the pale yellow and blue. Any light color can be used in a first coat background. When more than one color is used in the background, yellow is usually one of them. A background of only one color is effective and easy for a beginner.

When choosing background colors, refer to the color wheel (Color Plate I). Use colors from your main design or use their complements. Use their neighbor colors or use the three colors which represent the triad.

After applying first coat backgrounds by the process described in this chapter, you may try another method. The second method will be more difficult but has the advantage of giving truer finished colors, as the yellow is only applied where you want yellow to show. Yellow is not applied to the entire surface. Each added color is placed in its individual area. However, you should not have any sharp dividing line between colors. To achieve this effect, work as follows, while all the colors are wet. Clean the brush well and dip it in oil. Wipe it on your cloth to remove excess oil, then with a blending cross stroke, blend the color edges.

Second Backgrounding

After you have completed your second design coat on flowers and leaves and before you add stems it is time to apply a second background over the first fired background.

Use the same colors as in the first background, applying the identical color over color. Apply pale yellow first, blending over the blue of the first background and then, overlap the yellow with the other background colors. It is not necessary to coat the entire plate with yellow when applying a second background.

Using darker colors you may want to accent around some of the flowers over the yellow background with yellow-red, blood red or carnation. When not following specific instructions, you may pick up any red in the design and use it as the accent. For example, the yellow-red center on the forget-me-not suggests the possibility of accenting around the blossom with yellow-red. Another example would be the blood-red tips on the dogwood petals, which suggest accenting around the blossom with blood red. The yellow-brown in fruit leaves could be picked up in the background around the design.

Purple or ruby may be used around a design over blue. The purple and ruby will go on more smoothly if the blue is wet. Avoid padding in this case as it may give a grainy effect.

Dark green may be used over apple green. Darker blue may be used over baby blue. Ruby over pink around the design or at the base of a dresser piece, such as a perfume bottle, is most effective.

Make sure to blend your background colors only where they join. Also, be careful that your brush is clean before starting a new color. Your paints should be slightly thinner for the second background than for the first. Do not use too much oil on the brush and work your colors well into your brush before painting. When painting around the design, keep the heavy side of the brush toward the design and carefully shade in the colors. The brush should be very dry in order to prevent oil from creeping into the design.

The second background may be padded as the first.

Tips on Backgrounding

Brushing in the color around the design and leaving it unpadded will give an uneven effect which is very interesting. Lightly pad with your finger where the darker color ends to eliminate any dividing color line.

When doing an upright piece, keep the background darker toward the base.

When planning a background, keep a light background behind the darker flowers and leaves and put a touch of dark behind the light flowers.

Put the lighter colors toward the center of a plate and keep darker colors toward the outer edge, particularly where the design nears the edge of the china.

6

Color

The china painter's color wheel is identical to the standard color wheel with two exceptions.

First, the china color wheel has two distinct sets of red colors. Iron reds, which contain the mineral iron, and the gold reds, which contain gold. Gold reds are referred to as gold rose or gold colors.

Second, the color orange on the standard wheel is known in china painting as yellow-red.

Warm and Cool Colors

Look at the color wheel (Color Plate I). Red and yellow are considered warm, sunshine colors. Yellow-green and the rose colors possess some of the characteristics of warm colors. Violet is a balance between warm and cool and approaches neutral. Green is a mixture of warm and cool but is usually considered cool. Blue is cool. Blue-green and violet-blue are in the cool classification.

Contrast and Perspective

In china painting, contrast gives depth to the painting. A pale-yellow background shaded over with a touch of red or yellow-red around a blue or purple flower will give sunshine and contrast. Deep shading green applied to leaves where they appear under a warm colored flower will also give perspective and contrast.

Bright colors have more intensity and will appear closer. Colors that are grayed give depth and appear further away. Grayed colors are also shadow colors. Where petals and flowers overlap, apply a grayed color on the flower underneath. This will give the effect of raising the top flower. Shadow depth must not be too definite. Do not completely surround any light flower or flower clump with a dark cool color.

Complementary Colors

The color directly opposite a color on the wheel is its complement. Purple complements yellow, green complements red, and yellow-red complements blue, etc. The complement of a warm color is a cool one and vice versa. Any color placed next to its complement will intensify that color. This explains the shading of yellow-red around blue forget-me-nots and why the green leaves emphasize the color of roses and red berries.

Neighbor Colors

The color on either side of every color is its neighbor shade. Neighbor colors will blend well together. For example, purple blends well with the rose colors or the blues.

One exception to this rule is that the gold rose colors and the iron-red colors are not good neighbors and cannot be used together. On the color plate there is a fence between these colors. Rose colors will blend with their other neighbor, purple. The iron-reds will blend with yellow-red, although they are seldom used together.

The Triad

The three colors which represent the points of a triangle placed on the color wheel will make a harmonious combination. For example, purple, green and yellow-red. (Nature does it with the violet — green leaves, yellow-red pistil and purple flower.)

Monochrome

Monochrome is any design which is painted with a variation of several tones of the same color. It gives a soft, restful effect and is particularly attractive on dinnerware.

Tips on Color

In the firing process, the glaze softens on the china and absorbs the color. Paint must be applied in thin coats. If color is too heavy, the glaze will not completely absorb it and the color will chip or appear uneven after firing. Depth of color is obtained by applying successive coats of painting, firing after each coat.

The iridescent effect in china painting is achieved by applying darker colors over lighter colors. No other painting medium will give a similar effect. To get this iridescence, apply purple over blue, for example, or dark blue over light blue. Never use a dark color as a first coat of paint, either in the main design or in the background.

When applying the first background, pick up the light colors that have been used in the first coat of paint on flowers and leaves. Add pale-yellow for sunshine effect. When applying the second background, use the same color as in the first background. Apply darker colors to accent around the design, on the outer edge of a plate, or at the base of vases, jugs, or lamps. For example:

First background	Second background accents
Light blue	Deeper blue, blue-gray, blue-green, shading green, brown-green, ruby, purple.
Light yellow	Any iron red, (blood or carnation are good), yellow-red, yellow-brown, deeper yellow, brown.
Light pink	Blue, violet, ruby, purple, deep rose.
Light blue-green	Deeper blue-green, shading green, brown-green.
Light green	Shading green, brown-green

China paints are mineral colors. They come in powder form and also, premixed in jars or tubes. The powder is the least expensive and most commonly used. It is sold by the vial which is a container, not a measure. Advanced painters will find it more economical to buy their most used colors by the ounce.

The gold colors, which include pink, rose, violet, ruby and purple, contain gold and are the most expensive of china paints. They must be applied in thin coats and be well ground. Fat oil or flux, added sparingly to the color, will help if colors are gritty. Test as you mix.

Basic Color List

With so many colors available, and since each manufacturer names his own paints, there is often a variety of names for the same color. Beginners should refer to the color chart where all basic colors are shown. Note that some basic colors have unusual names. However, there are standard shades always available such as blood red, apple green, shading green, and Albert yellow.

Beginners should have a set of small plates on which to test the colors. Divide the test plate into pie-shaped sections with outlining ink. Put the name of the color in the center and add names and sources as you acquire them.

Initial colors required for beginners should include:

2 yellows	pale and medium shades
2 rose colors	pale pink, medium rose.
2 blues	pale blue, medium blue
2 blue-greens	pale and medium blue-green.
3 first coat greens	yellow-green, apple and blue-green
2 second coat greens	brown-green and darker or shading green
1 pure gray	
1 blood red	
1 true brown	
1 yellow-red	
1 yellow-brown	
1 purple	

China colors cannot all be intermixed. It will be helpful to study the following hints on mixing and to note some of the commercial names of the colors.

Iron Red

There is a large variety of reds available. Some require light firing and these are referred to as "light fire." Generally, the iron reds cannot be mixed in equal proportions with the gold colors because the gold color will predominate over the iron color. When necessary to mix, remember to add a larger ration of the iron color. For example, violet of iron is best bought commercially, but may be mixed from blood red and deep purple.

32

Shadow color for pink and rose flowers is made from lavender mixed with a touch of blood red.

Blood red is best purchased commercially; you will not obtain good results if you try to mix it yourself.

Iron reds over wet, unfired yellow will be partially consumed in the firing process. A fired yellow will lose most of its power to consume the iron red.

If you are mixing red with yellow or applying red over yellow, test fire first.

COMMERCIAL NAMES

Pale

Brilliant	Nasturtium
Chinese	Poppy
Christmas	Tomato
Holly red	

Medium

Carnation	
Light pompadour	Persian

Dark

Blood red	Dark pompadour
(one of the most	
commonly used reds)	

Yellow-red

This is one of the common colors and is made by every manufacturer. It should be purchased commercially. To lighten yellow-reds, apply over a fired pale yellow.

Light carnation   Yellow-red

Yellow

Pale yellow, referred to as ivory, is used frequently as a first coat background. Bright yellow over pale yellow is used in the second background.

Yellow is a warm, sunshine color and generally should be in every piece of naturalistic painting. Put bright yellow in the centers of flowers. A thin coat of pale yellow is often used as a first coat on a pink flower. Pale pink or rose should be applied over the wet yellow to shade the flower bowl and petals.

If yellow is applied too heavily, the china will be splotchy after firing. Any strong yellow, if mixed with red, will partially consume it in the firing process.

Be cautious when mixing yellow with reds and browns and test fire before using. Yellow-brown is better bought commercially.

COMMERCIAL NAMES

Pale

Ivory yellow   Trenton ivory
Neutral yellow   Trenton yellow
Primrose

Medium

Canary   Lemon

Dark

Albert   Egg

Yellow-Green

Pale

Eve   Sap
Moss

Dark

Chartreuse   Meissen
Dark yellow-green   Olive
                                       (contains a little brown)

Green

Mix with gray for a gray-green. Yellow mixed with a commercial blue-gray will also give a gray-green which is good for monochrome and shading white flowers. Dark green mixed with yellow-brown makes a brown-green which is commonly used in china painting. Brown-green may also be purchased commercially.

COMMERCIAL NAMES

Pale

Apple   Emerald
Bright

Medium

Empire   Royal
Grass

Dark

Black Green   Shading green
Brown Green   Velvet green
Dark green

35

Blue-green

Pale

Baby blue	Old Russian
(more blue than green)	Russian
Light blue-green	Water

Dark

Deep blue-green	Peacock
Deep Russian green	Persian
Emerald	(more blue than green)
Myrtle	Sultana

Blue

Easily mixes with purple, green, rose, or pink. It is better to purchase blues commercially. Blue mixed with pure gray gives a good shadow color and also is lovely for monochrome painting.

COMMERCIAL NAMES

Pale

Air	Light sky
Azure	Turquoise

Medium

Banding blue	Royal
Forget-me-not	Severs

Dark

Aztec	Dark blue
Copenhagen	Delft

Third
coat

IX. Flowering Dogwood Cake Plate

First coat

Second coat

VIII. Flowering Dogwood Design

The White Dogwood Design

(COLOR PLATES VIII AND IX)

The flowering dogwood, which is the state flower of Virginia and North Carolina, is one of the most popular designs in china painting. The blossom is actually a tiny cluster of flowers surrounded by four white leaves that look like petals.

This design is particularly appropriate for the larger china pieces. It looks well on cake platters, chop plates, casserole and buffet dishes. Tall lamps, vases and the larger pitchers and jugs can all be effectively done with the dogwood pattern. Put it on a cookie jar to make a pretty accent in the kitchen.

Colors as shown in color plate

First coat	Flowers — yellow centers
	Separate flowers with gray-green
	Leaves — Lemon yellow, apple green
Background	Pale yellow, pale blue green
Second coat	Separate petals with green-gray
	Detail in centers with brown-green
	Indentations of petals, blood red
	Leaves brown-green
Background	Blood red over yellow. Dark green shaded over blue green
Shadows	Gray with blood red mixed in

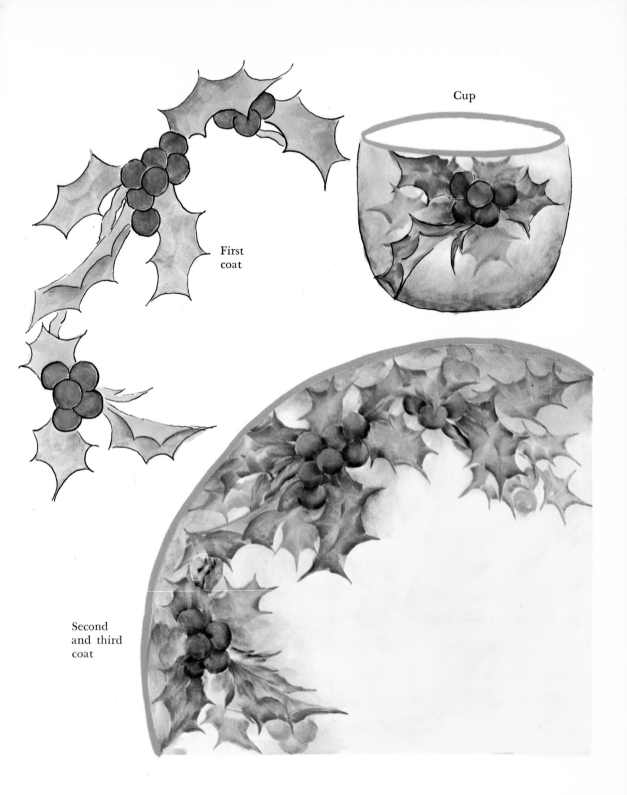

Cup

First
coat

Second
and third
coat

VII. Holly Design on Tom and Jerry Set

The Holly Design

The holly leaves have a glossy, leathery surface with spines along the edges. Clusters of bright red berries make the holly a gay and attractive design for china painters.

As a decoration, holly is as much a part of the Christmas season as the lighted evergreen tree. Gifts which you may do for friend and family have an extra touch when they are personalized with names and dates.

An entire set, either tea or coffee, painted with Christmas holly will make a dramatic picture on your serving table. Dessert and TV sets with the cups and plates are ideally suited for holly and are also unique.

For a festive holiday look, do a cigarette box with matching lighter and ash trays for your coffee table. Candlesticks with the larger bases will add greatly to your decorated mantel when they are hand painted with holly. The taller candy dishes are pretty with this design and for just an accent on your dinner table, the platters and cake plates are very festive done in holly patterns.

Colors as shown in color plate

First coat	Persian red on berries
	Leaves — yellow-green, blue-green
Background	Ivory and apple green
Second coat	Berries — shade with blood red
	Leaves — brown-green
Background	Blood red over ivory
	Shading green over apple green.
Third coat	Berries — blood red
	Leaves — shade with shading green
Shadows	Brown-green

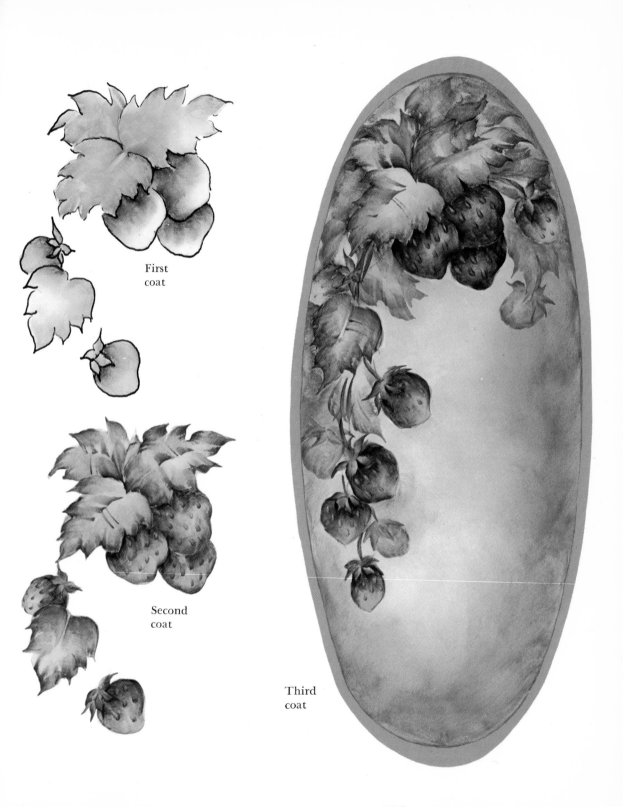

First
coat

Second
coat

Third
coat

VI. Strawberries on a Pickle Dish

The Strawberry Design

(COLOR PLATE VI)

The strawberry is a small plant which belongs to the rose family. It has a short, fuzzy stem and the leaves grow in groups of three. The berries are greenish white at first and turn to darker red as they ripen.

This design is informal and should be put on casual ware such as breakfast sets or kitchen pieces. Try it on children's dishes, jam jars and mugs. Cookie jars and fruit plates are nicely done with this design. For an unusual effect on your serving table, do a punch bowl with this design and fill with Christmas fruit punch for your holiday party.

Backgrounds can be varied. Use lots of yellow, yellow-browns and dark browns. In the second background, apply blood red over yellow.

Colors in color plate

First coat	Berries — ivory, blood red, yellow-green
	Leaves — lemon yellow, yellow brown, apple green
	Background — ivory, apple green
Second coat	Berries — blood red
	Leaves — brown-green
	Background — blood red over ivory, shading green over apple green
Third coat	Berries — blood red
	Leaves — dark green
	Shadows — brown-green

First coat

Second coat

Third coat

Juice glass

V. Yellow Daisy Juice Set

The Yellow Daisy Design

(Color Plate V)

The daisy is the state flower of Maryland and a member of the sunflower family. It is a sun-shaped flower, one blossom to each stem. Leaves are stiff and fuzzy, growing alternately one above the other on the stems.

This is an informal design good for juice sets or breakfast dishes. Cake plates and cookie jars and, particularly, flower vases of all sizes will look well with the daisy. In your den or recreation room lamps done with daisies give an informal yet attractive appearance.

Colors as shown in color plate

First coat	Centers — yellow-brown
	Leaves — yellow
Background	Pale yellow, apple green
Second coat	Petals — lemon yellow
	Center — finishing brown
Background	Yellow-red over light yellow
Shadows	Brown-green

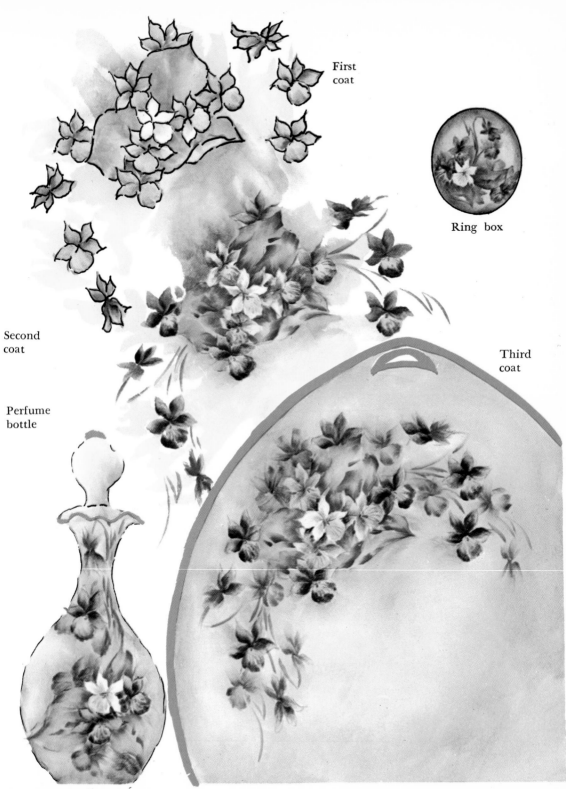

First coat

Ring box

Second coat

Third coat

Perfume bottle

IV. Violets on Dresser Tray

The Violet Design

(COLOR PLATE IV)

The violet is a five-petal flower which has heart-shaped leaves and very slender stems. It makes a light and dainty design which is particularly appropriate for any small china pieces.

Try this design on dresser sets. Include perfume bottles, pin trays, ring trees, small dresser trays and jewelry boxes.

Little boudoir lamps can be beautifully done with violet designs, also dainty vases and doorknobs. Or try it on light switch plates for a unique decoration.

If you are planning a particular gift using a state flower, the blue violet has been adopted as the state flower by Illinois, New Jersey, Rhode Island and Wisconsin.

Violets come in many colors although the blue and purple are the most popular.

Colors as shown in color plate

First coat	Flowers — lemon yellow, baby blue
	Leaves—lemon yellow, apple green
Background	Pale yellow, baby blue
Second coat	Flowers — dark purple, gray, yellow-red
	Leaves — brown green
Background	Yellow-red and purple
Third coat	Shadows — purple and blood red mixed

First coat

Cup

Second
and third
coat

III. Wild Rose Design for Tea and Toast Set

The Pink Wild Rose Design
(COLOR PLATE III)

The wild rose is a simple, five-petal flower which is one of the easiest designs for inexperienced china painters. New York originated the adoption of state flowers in 1891 by making the wild rose its state flower. It is also the state flower of North Dakota and Iowa.

Wild roses may be done in all sizes. Beginners should always do their initial painting on flat pieces such as tiles, trivets, all sizes of plates or wall plaques. More advanced painters can do dinnerware, all types of dresserware, coffee sets which include the pot, creamer, and sugar bowl, with cups and saucers. Rose jars and jam jars or compotes take this design well. Be sure to suit the size of your design to the size of your china piece.

Colors as shown in color plate

First coat	Pale pink on petals
	Yellow-green and blue-green on leaves
Background	Baby blue, light pink, pale yellow
Second coat	Light pink on petals
	Separate petals with pink-gray
Background	Leaves — brown-green; dark green over blue
Shadows	Pink, blue and blood red

Design for
dresser tray
or jewel box

First
coat

Third
coat

Second
coat

II. Apple Blossom Design for a Lamp

The Apple Blossom Design

(COLOR PLATE II)

The apple blossom is very like the wild rose in design. It is one of the simpler flowers and ideal for the beginner. The pink and white petals with the green leaves are the standard colors, and there is no common variation.

The apple blossom has been adopted as state flower by Arkansas and Michigan.

This design may be done in varying sizes. The larger apple blossoms make attractive platters, bread and sandwich trays, vegetable bowls and flower vases. Informal breakfast sets, tea and toast, TV, and snack sets all can be done effectively with the apple blossom. The larger lamps will also look well with this design.

Try the smaller apple blossom on egg cups, demi-tasse sets with small sugar and creamers to match. Coasters and condiment sets which include vinegar cruets, mustard pots, salt and peppers, and matching trays, all make up attractively with this design.

Colors as shown in color plate

First coat	Flowers — light pink
	Leaves — lemon yellow, apple green
Background	Pale yellow, pale pink, baby blue
Second coat	Flowers — pale pink, shade with pink-gray
	Leaves — brown-green
Background	Shading green at base of lamp
Third coat	Blood red dots
	Shading green at base of leaves
Shadows	Gray and strong rose

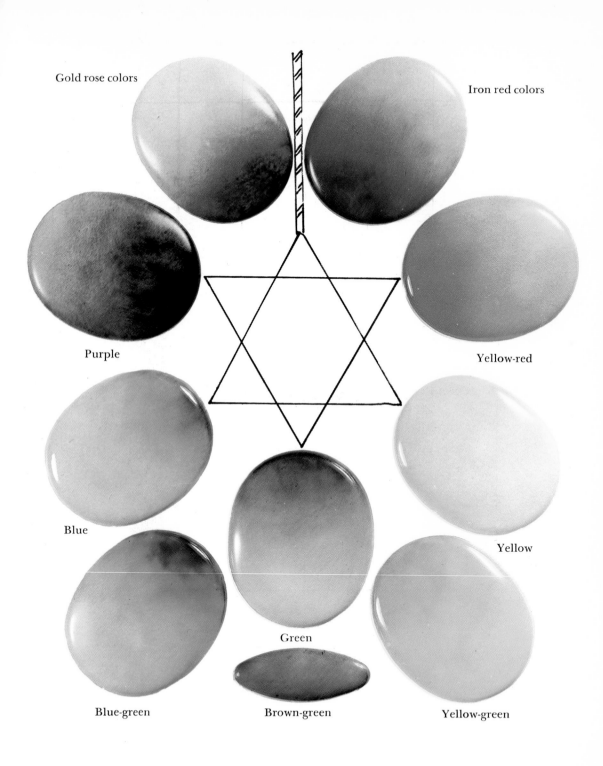

Gold rose colors

Iron red colors

Purple

Yellow-red

Blue

Yellow

Blue-green

Green

Brown-green

Yellow-green

I.   Color Wheel

Purple

This color shades from light violet to deep grape and black purple. To gray a purple, add a light green to violet, dark green to deeper tones. Purple mixed with black is often dull after firing.

COMMERCIAL NAMES

Pale

Blue violet	Pansy
Light violet of gold	Royal violet
Lilac	

Dark

Purple	Grape

Gold Rose Colors

Rose. This color will appear orangey if it is underfired. Overfired, it will take on a purple tint.

Pink and pale rose. These are good first-coat colors.

Gray-pink and rose-gray. Mix by adding apple green or gray to color. These are good shadow colors.

Strong rose. This is generally a second-coat color. Use it to brighten rose-colored flowers.

Ruby. This color tends to be gritty. It is usually a second- or third-coat color.

Ruby and maroon. These colors are almost identical. To gray, mix with dark green or gray. This color applies more easily over a wet coat of pale pink or rose. If mixed with black, it tends to be dull.

Ruby purple. This is usually a second- or third-coat color. It is good, used with ruby and rose as a shadow tone.

Pale

Apricot	Pink tint
Carmine	Shell pink
English pink	Soft pink
Peach blossom	Sweet pea pink

Medium

American beauty	Rose salmon
Deep pink	Strong rose
Rose	

Dark

Crimson purple	Ruby
Mauve	Ruby purple
Rich fuchsia rose	

Brown

This color is best purchased commercially and ranges from yellow-brown and red-brown to dark brown.

Hair or finishing brown	Red-brown
Okra	Yellow-brown

Gray

This color should be purchased commercially. Pure gray can be mixed with most colors. Mixed with blood red, it is a good shadow color. Mix it with yellow for shading white flowers. To make shading gray, add green of the same intensity to pinks and roses.

White

White as a china color may be mixed with most colors to lighten them. It is more desirable to apply color thinner to make a lighter tone. Test fire.

Black

This color is best purchased commercially. It tends to dull any color with which it is mixed.

Flux

This is a white powder sold by the ounce and in vials. It is used to fuse the color to the china; most china colors already have a small portion of flux mixed in. When gold colors are grainy, add flux, cautiously.

7

Apple Blossom Design

(Color Plate II; Figures 7-10)

a — Complete flower
b — Partial flower
c — Turned flower
d — Buds
e — Leaves
f — Baby leaves
g — Stems
h — Shadows

Figure 7

Step 1 — This is the master drawing for the apple blossom. Trace from this design and apply to a plate if desired. This is a good beginner's design as it is one of the simpler flowers.

When you do a smaller piece such as a jewelry box or small vase, trace from the color plate and follow the general instructions in this chapter.

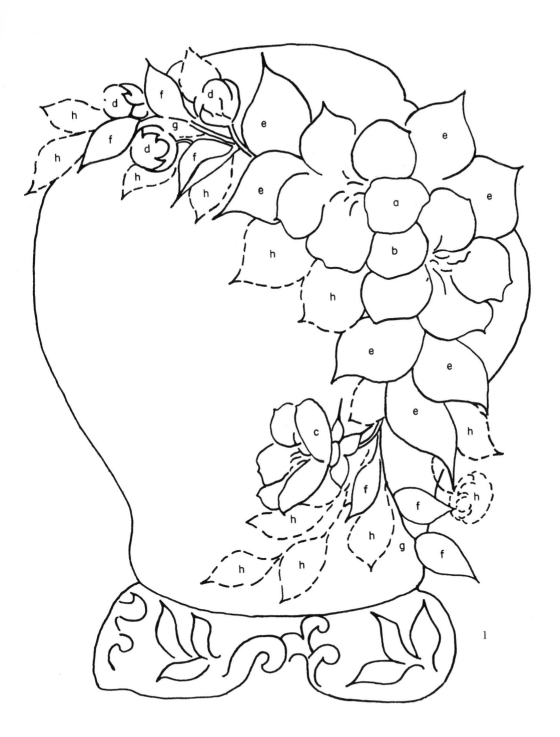

Fig. 7

First Coat

Trace design onto onionskin and transfer to china with graphite paper. Do not trace in shadows or stems. Mix light pink, apple green, lemon yellow, yellow-green. Use #8 brush throughout.

STEP 2 — Using comma stroke, shade halo above center of flower with yellow.

STEP 3 — Using corner stroke, paint into center with apple green.

STEP 4 — Using broken C stroke, lightly tip petals on turned flower with light pink. Keep heavy side of brush to outside of petal. Rotate china as you work. Fill lower petals completely with light pink. Pink *must* be very light and faint appearing. If there is any excess, roll your finger over it to remove surplus.

STEP 5 — Using broken C stroke, tip each petal with light pink. Rotate piece as you work and roll finger over pink to remove excess color.

STEP 6 — Fill buds with light pink.

STEP 7 — Fill calyx of buds with yellow-green.

STEP 8 — Fill ¾ of leaf surfaces with lemon yellow, stroking toward the tips.

STEP 9 — Fill baby leaves with lemon yellow.

STEP 10 — Using S stroke, tip baby leaves with yellow-green over the lemon yellow. This must be done while the yellow is still wet.

STEP 11 — Using S stroke, tip large leaves with yellow-green. This must be done while the yellow is still wet.

STEP 12 — Shade base of all leaves with apple green. Keep the heavy side of the brush in toward flower.

STEP 13 — Fill calyx of turned flower with yellow-green.

Background and First Firing

Mix pale yellow, baby blue, pale pink. With ½-inch brush, apply background as already explained. See color plate.

Blend and pad. Dry and fire.

2. yellow   3. apple   4. pink
green

6. pink

5. pink

7. yellow-
green

8. yellow

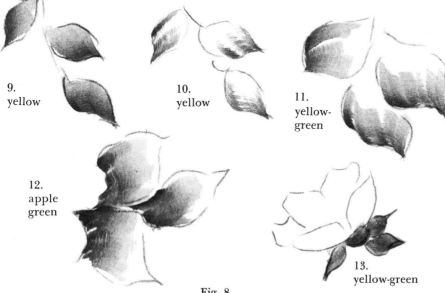

9.
yellow

10.
yellow

11.
yellow-
green

12.
apple
green

13.
yellow-green

Fig. 8

Second Coat

Retrace design on china. Do not trace on shadows. Mix pale pink, apple green, brown-green. Add a bit of apple green to pink to make a pinky gray.

STEP 14 — Using corner stroke, separate flowers with pink-gray.

STEP 15 — Using comma stroke, shade around each petal with pink-gray. Break strokes. Keep heavy side of brush toward the center.

STEP 16 — Using S stroke, outline other petals of the turned flower with pink-gray.

STEP 17 — Using corner stroke, put center in each flower with brown-green.

STEP 18 — Using broken comma stroke, shade base of each leaf with brown-green.

STEP 19 — Using S stroke, paint down center of turned leaf with brown-green.

STEP 20 — Using broken comma stroke, mark center of each leaf with brown-green.

STEP 21 — Using S stroke, shade each baby leaf with brown-green. With side of brush, add stems with brown-green.

STEP 22 — Using comma stroke, tip each large leaf with brown-green.

Second Background (Optional)

Intensify background colors and add any dark shading green to base of lamp and behind flowers, as in the color plate. Keep heavy side of brush toward flower.

Blend. Avoid padding if possible. Metallic trim may be added at this time following the special instructions in Chapter 3. Dry and fire second coat.

14. pink-gray

15. pink-gray

16. pink-gray

17. brown-green

18. brown-green

19 brown-green

20. brown-green

21. brown-green

22. brown-green

Fig. 9

Third Coat

Trace in shadows from onion skin using graphite paper. Mix brown-green, blood red; add a little gray to a strong rose for shadow color.

STEP 23 — Using the side of the #8 brush, or OO pointer, add center to each main flower with brown-green.

STEP 24 — Using OO pointer, put dots on each center with blood red.

STEP 25 — Using ½-inch brush, put base in shadow leaves with shadow color. Keep heavy side of brush toward the flower.

STEP 26 — Using ½-inch brush with broken comma stroke, tip shadow leaves lightly with shadow color.

STEP 27 — Using the side of #8 brush, add stems, using shadow color.

STEP 28 — With #8 brush, using broken S stroke, shade baby shadow leaves, using shadow color.

Add second application of metallic trim, if desired, following special instructions. Dry and fire third coat.

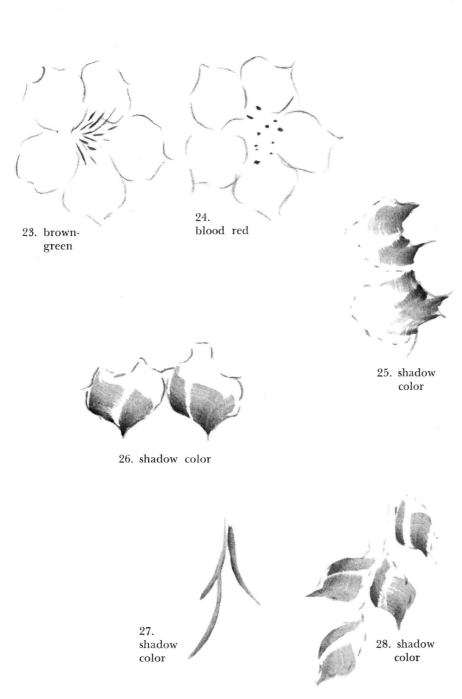

23. brown-
    green

24.
blood red

25. shadow
    color

26. shadow color

27.
shadow
color

28. shadow
    color

Fig. 10

8

The Pink Wild Rose Design

(Color Plate III; Figures 11-17)

a — Complete flower
b — Incomplete flower (note that one petal is partially covered by flower a)
c — Leaves underneath flowers
d — Isolated turned flower
e — Isolated buds
f — Baby leaves
g — Stems with thorns
h — Shadows

Figure 11

Step 1 — Trace from this design for any eight-inch plate, the TV plate and candy dishes. Reverse the right end of the design and trace onto a vase or jug. For smaller pieces, trace directly from the color plate and follow directions in this chapter.

Fig. 11

Figure 12

STEP 2 — Trace from this design for any average cup. The cup design may be traced from the color plate and applied to salt and peppers, small vases or demi-tasse sets.

50

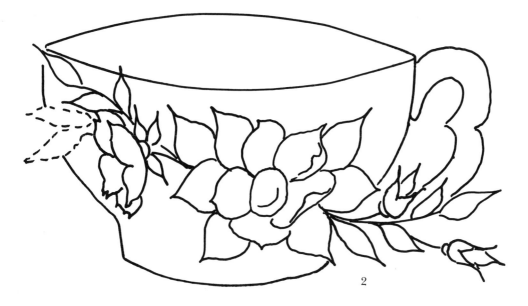

2

Fig. 12

First Coat

Trace design onto onionskin and apply to china piece using graphite paper. Do not include shadows or stems. Mix lemon yellow, blue-green, yellow-green, light pink

STEP 3 — With #8 brush, fill in centers with lemon yellow.

STEP 4 — With #8 brush, using C stroke, shade inner circle with yellow-green.

STEP 5 — With #8 brush, using C stroke, shade left side of three petals on the complete flower with light pink. Do not rotate piece for this stroke. Keep light pink very thin or it will appear orangey after firing.

STEP 6 — With #8 brush, using broken comma stroke, shade around center on the complete flower with light pink.

STEP 7 — With #8 brush, using corner stroke, shade partial petal with light pink. This separates the flowers. Keep the heavy side of the brush toward the complete flower.

STEP 8 — Turn china completely around so the buds are to your left. With #8 brush, using C stroke, shade four petals on the incomplete flower with light pink.

STEP 9 — With #8 brush, using broken comma stroke, shade around center on petal with light pink. Keep heavy side of brush toward centers.

52

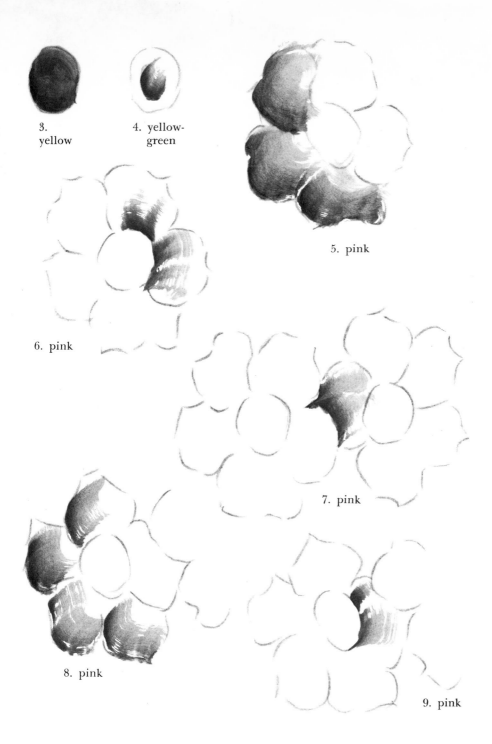

3.
yellow

4. yellow-
green

5. pink

6. pink

7. pink

8. pink

9. pink

Fig. 13

Step 10 — With #8 brush, using long C stroke, shade base of isolated turned flower with light pink.

Step 11 — With #8 brush, using corner stroke, paint center of isolated, turned flower with yellow-green.

Step 12 — With #8 brush, fill in from center to edge on top petals of isolated, turned flower with light pink. Keep the pink light. Roll finger over pink to remove any excess. Do not cover yellow-green applied in Step 11.

Step 13 — With #8 brush, fill in bud centers with light pink.

Step 14 — With #8 brush, fill in tips and centers of all large leaves with lemon yellow.

Step 15 — With #8 brush, using S stroke, paint baby leaves with lemon yellow. Do not paint in stems.

Step 16 — With #8 brush, outline around flowers at base of all leaves with blue-green. Keep heavy side of brush toward the flower. Blend color divisions so there is no harsh line.

Step 17 — With #8 brush, fill in calyx of isolated flower with blue-green.

Step 18 — With #8 brush, using broken S stroke, paint down left side of some leaves with yellow-green. See color plate. This must be done while the lemon yellow is still wet.

Step 19 — With #8 brush, using small C stroke, fill in calyx of buds with blue-green.

Backgrounding and First Firing

Mix pale yellow, light pink, baby blue. Use more oil when applying pink, keep it thin as it doubles in intensity during firing.

With ½-inch brush, apply background as already explained. Blend and pad. Dry and fire first coat.

54

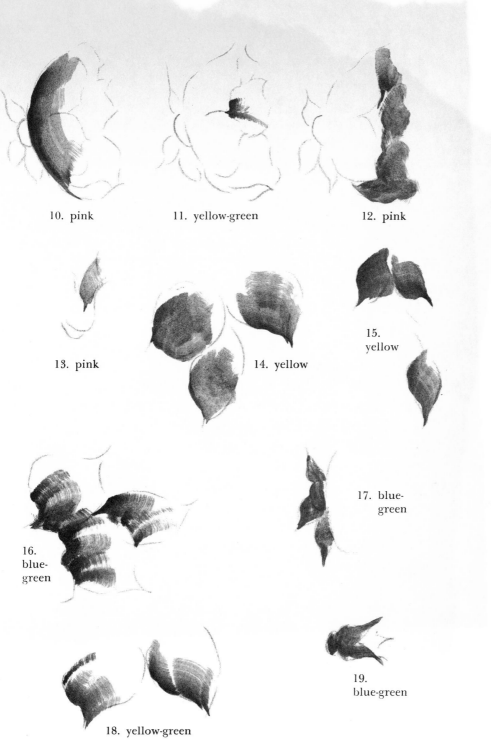

10. pink   11. yellow-green   12. pink

13. pink   14. yellow

15. yellow

16. blue-green

17. blue-green

18. yellow-green

19. blue-green

Fig. 14

Second Coat

Retrace design on china but do not include shadows. Mix light pink, brown-green, add apple green to pink to make pink-gray mixture; add a little dark purple to blood red to make violet of iron. Use extra oil when applying pink. Keep it thin and well shaded. It doubles in intensity during firing.

STEP 20 — With #8 brush, using C and comma strokes, intensify all petals with pink.
STEP 21 — With #8 brush, using broken comma stroke, lightly separate petals with pink-gray. Rotate china as you work.
STEP 22 — With #8 brush, using corner stroke, separate flowers with gray. Keep heavy side of the brush toward complete flower.
STEP 23 — With #8 brush, using long S stroke, paint turned petals gray.
STEP 24 — With #8 brush, using broken stroke, lightly shade through center of turned isolated flower with gray.
STEP 25 — With #8 brush, using comma stroke, separate petals on the turned, isolated flower with gray.
STEP 26 — With #8 brush, using long S stroke, shade turned petal on the turned isolated flower with gray.

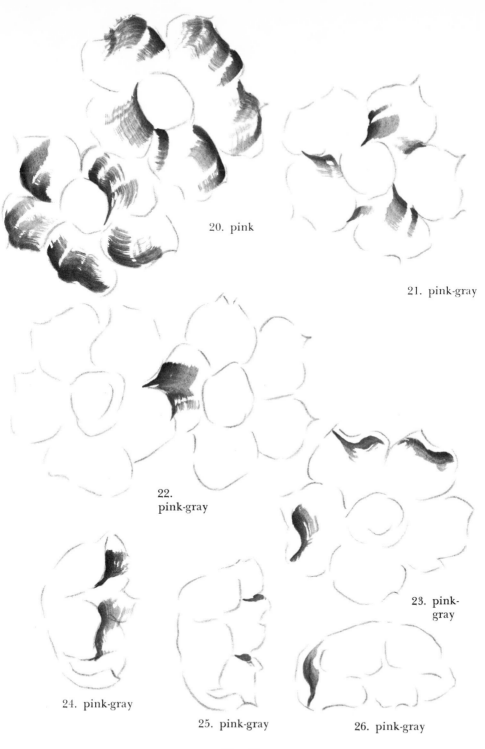

20. pink

21. pink-gray

22.
pink-gray

23. pink-
gray

24. pink-gray

25. pink-gray

26. pink-gray

Fig. 15

Step 27 — With #8 brush, using long S stroke, paint through centers of buds with pink-gray.

Step 28 — With #8 brush, using C stroke, shade centers of flowers with brown-green. Keep brush well spread.

Step 29 — With #8 brush, using small C stroke, shade inside centers of flowers with brown-green.

Step 30 — With #8 brush, shade base of all leaves with brown-green. Keep heavy side of brush toward flower.

Step 31 — With #8 brush, using broken comma stroke, make centers in leaves with brown-green.

Step 32 — With leaf tip pointing down, use #8 brush and broken comma stroke to tip each leaf with violet of iron.

Step 33 — With #8 brush, using broken S stroke, shade each baby leaf with violet of iron.

Step 34 — With #8 brush, using small C stroke, shade base of calyx on isolated turned flower with brown-green.

Step 35 — With #8 brush, using S stroke, paint balance of calyx of isolated, turned flower with brown-green.

Step 36 — With #8 brush, using small C stroke, paint base of bud calyx with brown-green.

Step 37 — With #8 brush, using large C stroke, paint bowl of bud calyx with brown-green.

Step 38 — Turn piece so bud points down. With #8 brush, using long S stroke, shade each side of calyx with brown-green.

Step 39 — With side of #8 brush, paint stems brown-green.

Step 40 — With #8 brush tip, using small comma stroke, add thorns with violet of iron.

Second Background (Optional)

Mix pale yellow, light pink, baby blue, any dark shading green. Intensify colors, particularly around design. Shade green over blue on edge of plate and at base of cup. Blend and pad.

Metallic trim may be applied following special instructions in Chapter 3.

Put gold or trim on handle of cup. Dry and fire second coat.

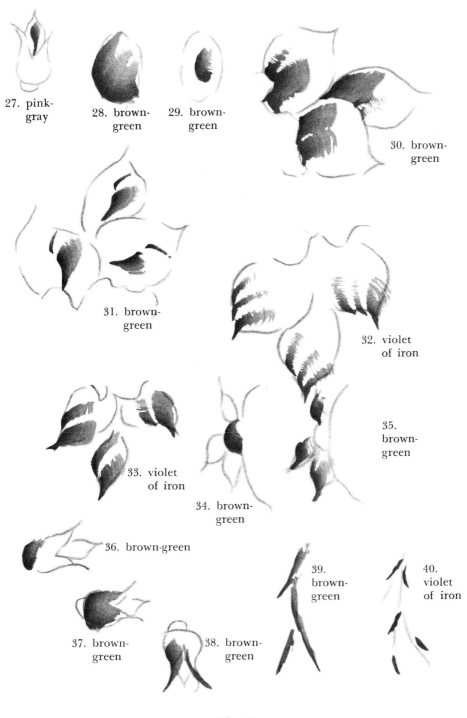

27. pink-gray

28. brown-green

29. brown-green

30. brown-green

31. brown-green

32. violet of iron

33. violet of iron

34. brown-green

35. brown-green

36. brown-green

37. brown-green

38. brown-green

39. brown-green

40. violet of iron

Fig. 16

Third Coat

Trace in shadows which are dotted on the original design. Mix brown-green, blood red, pink, blue. To make shadow mixture, mix ratio of nine-tenths pink and blue combined, and add one-tenth blood red (pink and blue make lavender).

STEP 41 — With side of #8 brush, using short broken stroke, add stamens with brown-green.

STEP 42 — With OO pointer, add big dots to tips of stamens and around back of center in an irregular pattern in blood red.

STEP 43 — With OO pointer, add stamens with brown-green and dots on isolated turned flower in blood red.

STEP 44 — With #8 brush, outline next to design at base of shadow leaves with shadow mixture.

STEP 45 — With #8 brush, using broken S stroke, put in tips of shadow leaves with shadow mixture. Keep brush well spread.

STEP 46 — With side of #8 brush, using a broken stroke, add shadow stems with shadow mixture.

STEP 47 — With #8 brush, using S stroke, put in small leaves with shadow mixture. Add second application of gold or other metallic trim, following the special instructions.

Dry and fire third coat.

Color Variation

You may substitute the following colors to make a *yellow* wild rose if desired. Follow the same procedure as outlined in the text.

First coat	Pale yellow on petals.
	Yellow-green and Albert yellow on leaves.
Background	Yellow-green, apple green, pale yellow.
Second coat	Lemon yellow on petals.
	Separate petals with yellow-grown and brown-green mixture.
Third coat shadows	Gray-violet mixture.

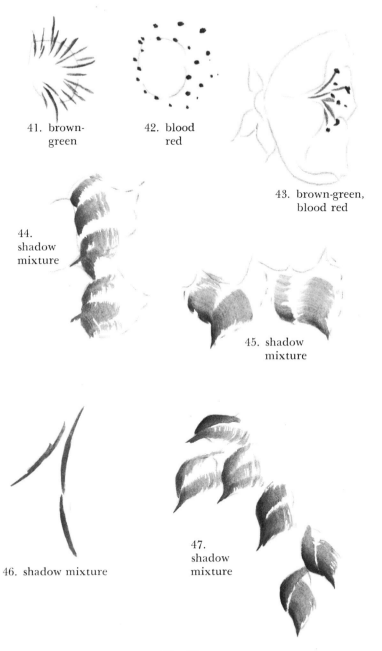

41. brown-
    green

42. blood
    red

43. brown-green,
    blood red

44.
shadow
mixture

45. shadow
    mixture

46. shadow mixture

47.
shadow
mixture

Fig. 17

9

Violet Design

(COLOR PLATE IV; FIGURES 18-22)

a — Completely outlined flower is the topmost one. It is the white flower in the color plate

b — These are incomplete flowers. Note that some petals are underneath other flowers

c — These are leaves underneath flowers. They partially cover blossoms

d — These are flowers partially covered by leaves

e — Isolated flowers

f — Isolated buds

g — Stems

h — Shadows

Figure 18

STEP 1 — Trace from this design for any flat tray or dish. It is most important to keep your first coat of blue on the flowers very thin. The second coat of purple applied over the blue must also be very thin. If deep color is desired, an extra firing is advisable. Refer to the color plate while painting.

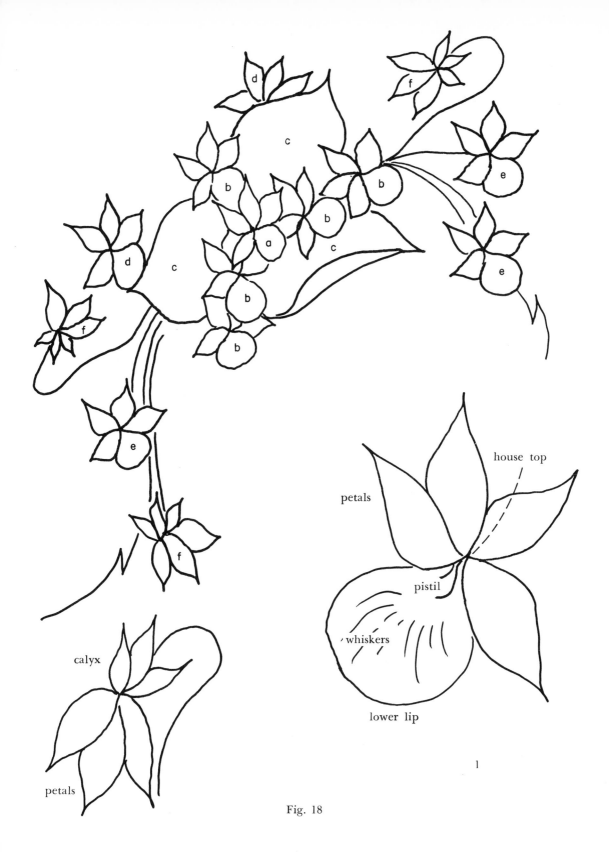

Fig. 18

Figure 19

S<small>TEP</small> 2 — Here is the violet design adapted for a lamp base and for small boxes from a dresser set.

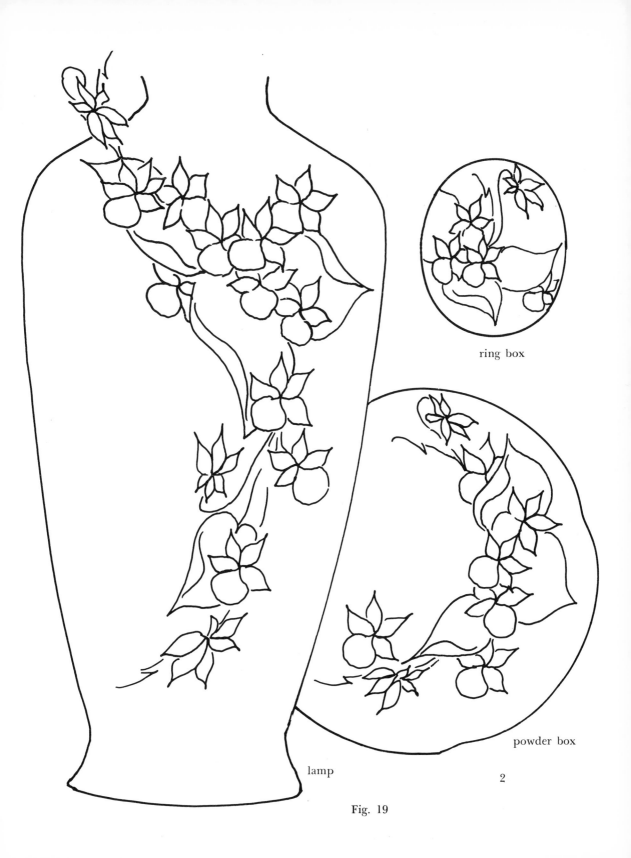

ring box

powder box

lamp

2

Fig. 19

First Coat

Trace design from this text on to onionskin paper and transfer to china with graphite paper. Do not trace shadows or stems. Mix baby blue, lemon yellow, apple green.

STEP 3 — With #8 brush, using corner stroke, paint lower lip of each violet with lemon yellow.

STEP 4 — Dip corner of brush in oil. Using corner stroke, shade flowers with baby blue where they overlap. Leave center flower white and keep flowers nearest the center lighter in color by applying the paint more lightly.

STEP 15 — Using S stroke, paint each petal of isolated flowers with baby blue.

STEP 6 — Using broken C stroke, paint outer edge of lower lip with baby blue on all flowers where the lower lip is complete.

STEP 7 — Using comma stroke, lightly shade each partial petal of flowers with baby blue. Keep flowers toward center lighter.

STEP 8 — Using S stroke, paint three large lower petals of the buds with baby blue.

STEP 9 — Using small S stroke, paint bud calyx with apple green.

STEP 10 — Color lower side of each leaf with lemon yellow.

STEP 11 — Keeping the heavy side of the brush to the outer edge, outline under flowers and cover balance of leaves with apple green.

Backgrounding and First Firing

Mix pale yellow and baby blue. With ½-inch brush, apply background as already explained. See color plate. Blend and pad. Dry and fire first coat.

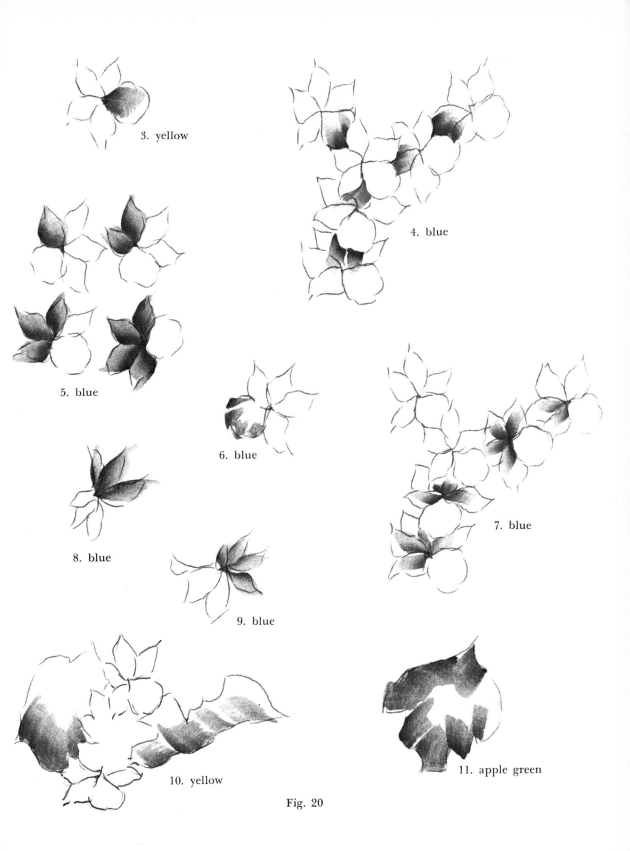

3. yellow

4. blue

5. blue

6. blue

7. blue

8. blue

9. blue

10. yellow

11. apple green

Fig. 20

Second Coat

Retrace design on piece. Do not trace in shadows. Mix dark purple, yellow-red, gray and brown-green.

STEP 12 — With #8 brush, using corner stroke, shade flowers with dark purple where they overlap. Central flower remains white. Apply paint more thinly on flowers nearest center so as to keep them lighter.

STEP 13 — Using S stroke and C stroke, shade petals and lower lips with dark purple on all flowers where any portion is complete.

STEP 14 — Using comma stroke, shade partial flower centers with purple.

STEP 15 — Using comma stroke, shade center of white flower with gray. Using C stroke, touch gray to lower lip.

STEP 16, 17 — With OO pointer, make light broken lines with purple to put whiskers on lower lip. Wash pointer in turpentine. Add pistil in center with yellow-red.

STEP 18 — Lightly apply a small housetop with brown-green.

STEP 19 — With #8 brush, using S stroke, paint three large petals of buds with purple.

STEP 20 — Using the corner of the brush and S stroke, paint bud calyx with brown green.

STEP 21 — With ½-inch brush, outline around flowers at the base of leaves, with brown-green. Keep heavy side of brush toward flower and break your strokes.

STEPS 22, 23 — Using broken comma stroke for centers and C stroke for sides, paint leaves with brown-green (turn plate for sides so leaves point downward). Using comma stroke, paint tips with brown-green.

STEP 24 — With #8 brush, using long S stroke, paint turned leaf with brown-green.

STEP 25 — With a broken stroke, add stems with brown-green. Use the edge of the brush.

(continued on page 70)

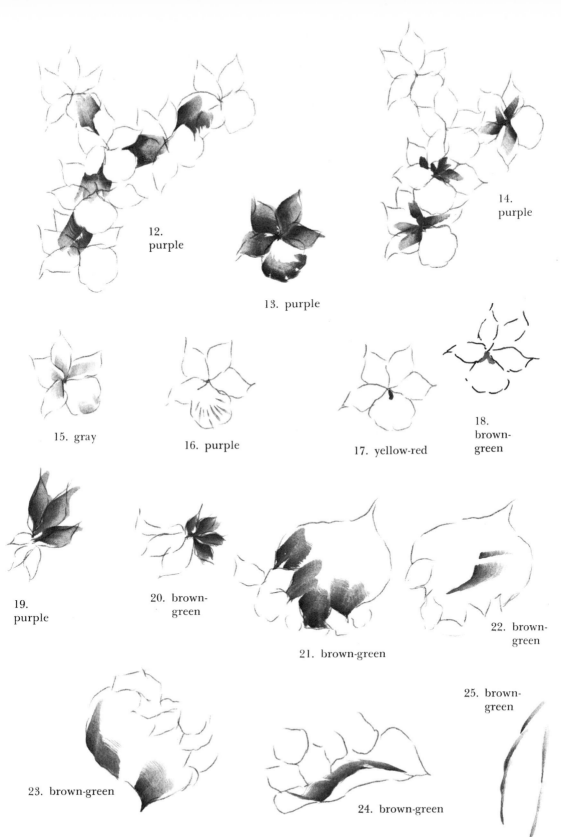

12.
purple

13. purple

14.
purple

15. gray

16. purple

17. yellow-red

18.
brown-
green

19.
purple

20. brown-
green

21. brown-green

22. brown-
green

23. brown-green

24. brown-green

25. brown-
green

Fig. 21

Second Background (Optional)

Mix yellow-red and purple. Apply yellow-red over light yellow and purple over blue around flowers, as in color plate. Blend and pad.

A gold or metallic rim may be added at this time following the special instructions in Chapter 3. Dry and fire second coat.

Third Coat

Mix purple and blood red in ratio of nine tenths purple to one tenth blood red. Add blood red to purple until desired shade is reached.

STEP 26 — Trace in shadows from onionskin tracing using graphite paper.

STEP 27 — With #8 brush, use comma stroke to intensify centers of violets with purple.

STEP 28 — Using broken S stroke, put in shadow petals with shadow paint.

STEP 29 — Using broken C stroke, paint lower lips of shadow flowers.

STEP 30 — Using broken S, put petals on shadow buds.

STEP 31 — Using small comma stroke, put calyx on bud shadows.

STEP 32 — With the edge of #8 brush, add stems. Turn china as you work so stems can be gracefully curved. Add second application of gold or metallic trim if desired. Dry and fire third coat.

Color Variation

First coat	Flowers — medium rose; leaves — lemon yellow
Background	Pale yellow and baby blue
Second coat	Flowers — ruby or violet gold, pale purple
	Leaves — any dark shading green
Second background	Carnation red over light yellow, ruby or violet of gold over blue
Shadows	Violet of gold, with a touch of blood red, or gray with a touch of blood red

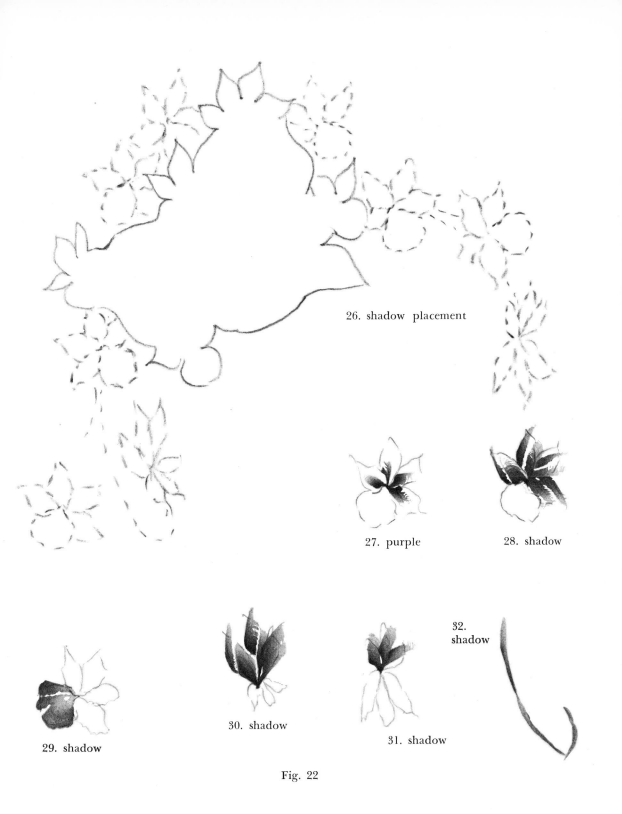

26. shadow placement

27. purple

28. shadow

29. shadow

30. shadow

31. shadow

32. shadow

Fig. 22

10

Yellow Daisy Design

(Color Plate V; Figures 23-28)

a — Complete flower
b — Incomplete flower (note three petals are partially covered by complete flower)
c — Partial isolated flower
d — Isolated buds
e — Leaves underneath flowers
f — Isolated leaves
g — Stems
h — Shadows

Figure 23

Step 1 — This is the master drawing for applying a yellow daisy onto a pitcher. For a smaller pitcher or for salt and pepper sets, trace design from the color plate.

72

1

Fig. 23

Figure 24

STEP 2 — A small portion of the yellow daisy design fits well on a juice glass, as shown here.

74

2

Fig. 24

First Coat

Trace design on to onionskin paper and apply to china piece with graphite paper. No shadows or stems are applied. Mix pale yellow, yellow-brown, yellow-green.

STEP 3 — With #8 brush, fill in centers of all flowers with yellow-brown.

STEP 4 — With #8 brush, fill in petals of all flowers with pale yellow.

STEP 5 — With #8 brush, using C stroke, shade over petals around center on partial, isolated flower with yellow-green. This must be done while yellow is still wet.

STEP 6 — With #8 brush, shade around centers on two other flowers with yellow-green. Keep heavy side of brush toward centers. This must be done while pale yellow is wet. Rotate china as you stroke.

STEP 7 — With #8 brush, fill in all leaves and buds with yellow-green.

Backgrounding and First Firing

Mix pale yellow, yellow-green, yellow-brown. With ½-inch brush, apply background as already explained. See color plate.

Blend and pad. Dry and fire first coat.

76

3. yellow-
   brown

4. pale-yellow

5. yellow-
   green

6. yellow-green

7. yellow-
   green

Fig. 25

Second Coat

Retrace design on china. Do not trace on shadows, or stems. MIX dark brown, yellow-red, brown-green.

STEP 8 — With #8 brush, using C stroke, shade centers with dark brown. Keep heavy side of brush toward the outside of centers. Rotate china as you stroke.

STEP 9 — With #8 brush, shade around center of each flower with brown-green. Keep heavy side of brush in toward center. Rotate china as you work.

Outline complete flower with brown-green to emphasize separation between flowers. Keep the heavy side of the brush toward the complete flower.

STEP 10 — With #8 brush, shade base of all leaves with brown-green. Keep heavy side of brush toward flowers.

STEP 11 — With #8 brush, using comma stroke, paint base of leaf segments with brown-green.

STEP 12 — With #8 brush, using S stroke, paint leaf tips with brown-green.

STEP 13 — With #8 brush, using small C stroke, paint base of each bud with brown-green. With #8 brush, using large C stroke, paint around each bud with brown-green. Rotate china as you work. With #8 brush, using two large C strokes, shade base of isolated leaves with brown-green.

STEP 14 — With #8 brush, using S stroke, paint tips of isolated leaf segments with brown-green.

Second Background (Optional)

Mix yellow-red, yellow-green, dark brown, yellow-brown. Apply yellow-red over pale yellow where shown. Intensify yellow-green and yellow-brown.

Apply dark brown over yellow-brown at base of china if desired. Blend. Do not pad, as a choppy effect is desirable. Metallic trim may be added at this time following the special instructions in Chapter 3. Dry and fire second coat.

8. dark brown

9. brown-green

10. brown-green

11. brown-green

12. brown-green

13. brown-green

14. brown-green

Fig. 26

Third Coat

Mix brown-green, dark brown and lemon yellow. Trace in shadows from onionskin, using graphite paper.

STEP 15 — With side of #8 brush, stroke in stems with brown-green.

STEP 16 — With #8 brush, intensify centers with dark brown if desired.

STEP 17 — With #8 brush, using broken, straight stroke, tip each petal of isolated flower with lemon yellow. Keep the heavy side of brush toward the outer edge of petal.

STEP 18 — With #8 brush, using broken, straight stroke, tip other petals lemon yellow.

STEP 19 — With #8 brush, using comma stroke, shade between petals of all flowers where needed, with brown-green.

STEP 20 — With ½-inch brush, using a very loose S stroke, lightly fill in shadows with brown-green. Add second application of gold, if desired, following special instructions. Dry and fire third coat.

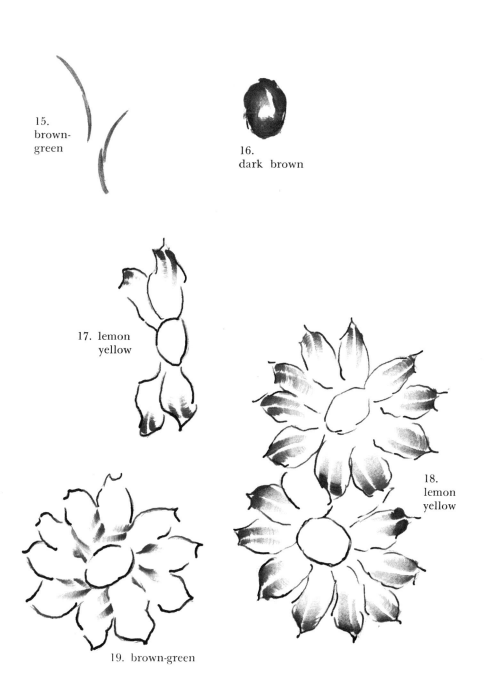

15.
brown-
green

16.
dark brown

17. lemon
yellow

18.
lemon
yellow

19. brown-green

Fig. 27

Color Variation

First coat	Centers in lemon yellow
	Leaves in lemon yellow and yellow green
Background	Pale yellow, apple green, yellow-brown
Second coat	Petals in green-gray
	Centers in yellow-red
Background	Yellow-red over light yellow
	Brown-green over yellow-green
Shadows	Green-gray

20

Fig. 28

11

Strawberry Design

(Color Plate VI; Figures 29-32)

a — Partial berries under leaf
    clump
b — Isolated whole berry
c — Complete leaves
d — Partial leaves
e — Stems
f — Shadows

Figure 29

Step 1 — This is the master drawing for strawberries on a pickle dish. You may trace from this design and put it also on an eight-inch plate. Take the lower berries on the left side and transfer them to the right side. Refer to the color plate as you work. Keep colors smooth and thin, adding extra coats if the desired depth of color is not obtained.

Fig. 29

First Coat

Trace design onto onionskin and apply to china with graphite paper. Do not trace in shadows or stems. Mix ivory, blood red, yellow-green, lemon yellow, yellow-brown, apple green. Use either #10 or ½-inch brush unless otherwise specified.

STEP 2 — Lightly coat three large partial berries with ivory. It is not necessary to shade.

STEP 3 — While ivory is still wet, shade top of berries with blood red. There should not be any dividing line between ivory and blood red. Blend division with finger. Keep the heavy side of brush to the top of berry.

STEP 4 — Coat small complete berries with ivory, two or three only at a time. Ivory will then still be wet when balance of color is added, as instructed in Steps 5, 6.

STEP 5 — With #8 brush over the wet ivory, shade top of each berry with blood red. Keep heavy side of brush to the top of berry.

STEP 6 — With #8 brush over wet ivory, shade tip of each whole berry lightly with yellow-green.

STEP 7 — Coat main clump of leaves with ivory. Over the wet ivory, shade tip of lower leaf with apple green. Using broken stroke, shade base of other leaves, where they overlap, with apple green.

STEP 8 — Turn piece around. Shade base of complete leaves with yellow-brown. Shade tips of other two leaves with yellow-brown.

STEP 9 — Coat small complete leaves with ivory. Shade outer edges with apple green. Rotate piece as you work.

STEP 10 — With #8 brush, paint in hulls of all whole berries with apple green.

Backgrounding and First Firing

Mix ivory, apple green. With ½-inch brush, apply background as already explained (red will be added later). See color plate. Blend and pad. Dry and fire.

86

2.
ivory

3.
blood
red

4.
ivory

5.
blood
red

6.
yellow-green

7. ivory
and
apple green

8.
yellow-
brown

9. ivory,
apple green

10.
apple green

Fig. 30

Second Coat

Retrace design on piece. Do not trace in shadows. Mix brown-green, blood red.

Step 11 — With #10 brush, outline each berry in the main clump, with blood red. Keep heavy side of the brush to the outside of berry and break stroke frequently. Color should be lightest at the base of berries and darkest where they overlap. The whole of the berry should not be covered with color.

Step 12 — With #4 brush over the wet blood red, make eight to ten tiny C strokes with the curved portion of the C to the base of the berry (this makes seed holes).

Step 13 — Do not wash brush in turpentine, but wipe clean and dip in oil. Using the same stroke as in Step 12 and while color is still wet on seed holes, wipe out center of seed holes with oily brush.

Step 14 — With #8 brush, using S stroke, tip leaves with brown-green. Using comma stroke, connect tips of all leaves with brown-green. It is not necessary to tip each section of every leaf. Undercoat should be partially showing.

Step 15 — With #8 brush, using broken comma stroke, add centers to leaves with brown-green. Be sure paint is shaded. Holding the brush straight up, add two straight marks to centers with brown-green. With #10 brush, separate leaves in main clumps where they overlap, with brown-green. Keep heavy side of brush toward the complete leaf.

Step 16 — With #10 brush, make two C strokes for base of leaf with brown-green. Keep heavy side of the brush to top of leaf. Leave a light streak in the middle. Turn piece around and with comma stroke, put tips on small leaves with brown-green.

Step 17 — With #10 brush, using small S stroke, shade one side of each finger on each hull of the isolated berries with brown-green. Tilt brush so you are only using a partial tip of the brush to make the stroke.

(continued on page 90)

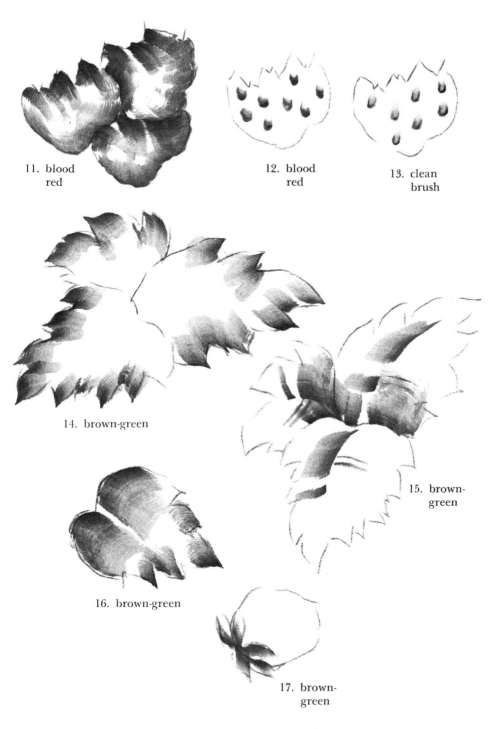

11. blood
    red

12. blood
    red

13. clean
    brush

14. brown-green

15. brown-
    green

16. brown-green

17. brown-
    green

Fig. 31

Second Background (Optional)

Darken colors in first background and blend blood red over ivory, dark green over apple green in the areas shown in the color plate. Blend. Do not pad. A choppy effect is desirable. Metallic trim may be added at this time following the specific instructions in Chapter 3. Dry and fire.

Third Coat

Trace in shadows from onionskin, using graphite paper. Trace in stems. Mix blood red, shading green, brown-green.

STEP 18 — With #8 brush, lightly shade outer edge of berries where needed with blood red. Darken where berries overlap.

STEP 19 — With #4 brush, darken and wipe out seed holes where needed with blood red.

STEP 20 — With #8 brush, using broken stroke, outline top of shadows with brown-green. Keep heavy side of brush to the outside edge.

STEP 21 — With #8 brush, using S stroke, put in tips of shadow leaves with brown-green.

STEP 22 — With #8 brush, using sharp comma stroke, connect between points of shadow leaves with brown-green.

STEP 23 — With #8 brush, lightly shade tip of shadow berries with brown-green. Keep heavy side of the brush to the outside edge.

STEP 24 — With #8 brush, using small S stroke, lightly shade hulls of shadow berries with brown-green, stroking from outer edge toward center.

STEP 25 — With #10 brush outline backs of complete leaves in main clump with shading green.

STEP 26 — Using the side of #8 brush, add all main stems and shadow stems with brown-green.

Add second application of gold, if desired, following special instructions. Dry and fire.

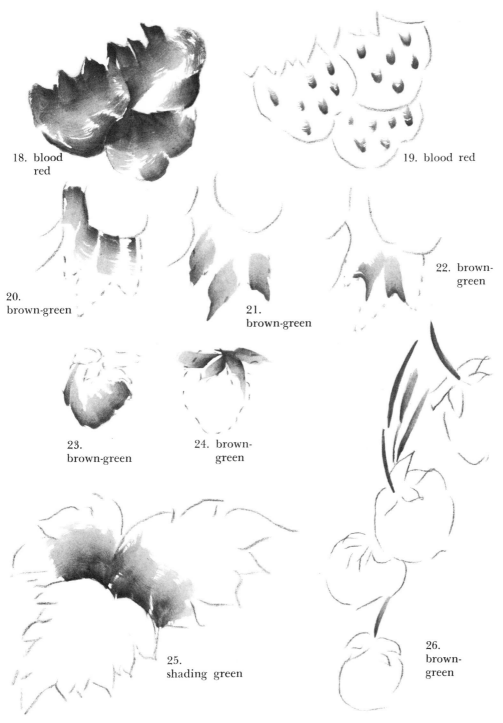

18. blood red

19. blood red

20. brown-green

21. brown-green

22. brown-green

23. brown-green

24. brown-green

25. shading green

26. brown-green

Fig. 32

12

Holly Design

(Color Plate VII; Figures 33-36)

a — whole berries
b — Incomplete berries. Note that partial berries are covered by whole berries or leaves
c — Leaves
d — Turned leaves
e — Branch
f — Shadows

Figure 33

Step 1 — This is the master design for using on the bowl of a Tom and Jerry set, or on any large plate. The design on the cup, which is illustrated in the color plate, is the lower berry clump. If there is no design applied to the outside of the bowl, cover the bowl with an apple green background.

In applying the design on the bowl, repeat the design three times on the inside and/or outside of the bowl. Use same design on small eight-inch plates, cups and saucers.

If a smaller design is needed, trace from the color plate.

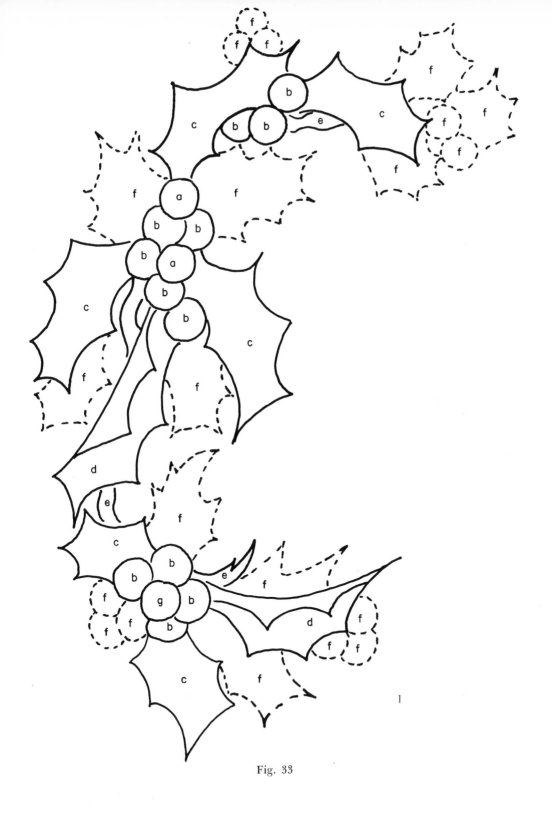

Fig. 33

First Coat

Trace design onto onionskin and transfer to china piece with graphite paper. Do not trace in shadows. Mix Persian red, yellow-green, blue-green. Before starting, it will be necessary to test the reds. You will need a light iron red such as Persian on your first coat of berries, and a dark iron red such as blood red on the second coat. Many times a dark red will completely consume the lighter red under it in firing. For this reason, test fire the light red, apply the dark red over it and fire again to be sure the dark red does not distort the undercoat.

STEP 2 — Use #8 brush throughout except where specified otherwise. Coat all berries with Persian red.

STEP 3 — Coat small leaves with yellow-green.

STEP 4 — Coat all two-tone leaves with yellow-green. While yellow is still wet, shade blue-green on top edges. Keep the heavy side of the brush toward the outside of the leaf.

STEP 5 — Coat all turned leaves with yellow-green. Shade through center, where leaf is turned, with blue-green.

STEP 6 — Coat all branches with yellow-green.

Backgrounding and First Firing

Mix pale yellow, apple-green. With ½-inch brush, fill center areas with pale yellow. Blend outer edges with apple green. Blend and pad. Dry and fire.

94

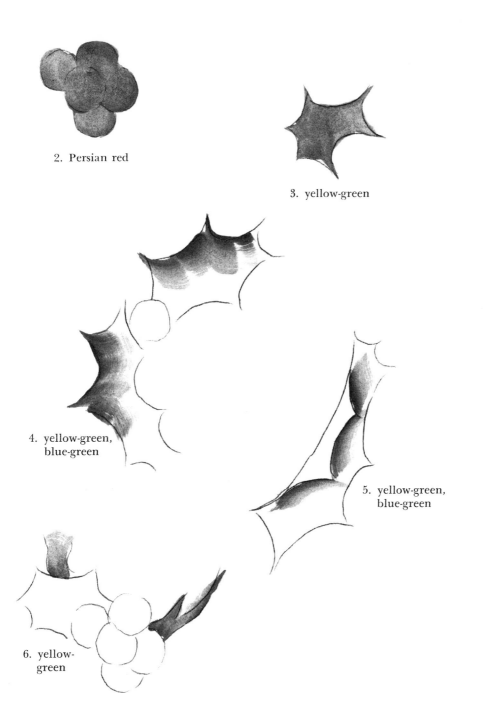

2. Persian red

3. yellow-green

4. yellow-green,
   blue-green

5. yellow-green,
   blue-green

6. yellow-
   green

Fig. 34

Second Coat

Retrace design on piece. Do not trace on shadows. Mix blood red, brown-green.

STEP 7 — With #4 brush, completely outline around whole berries with blood red. Keep the heavy side of the brush toward berry.

STEP 8 — With #4 brush, using comma stroke, separate berries with blood red. Keep the heavy side of the brush toward the berry.

STEP 9 — With #4 brush, using C stroke, shade lower edge of berries toward, with blood red.

STEP 10 — With #8 brush, practice making a comma stroke with a pointed tip.

STEP 11 — Using the above stroke, go around outer edge of each leaf with brown-green, giving the spiked effect.

STEP 12 — With #8 brush, shade turned leaves with brown-green.

STEP 13 — With #4 brush, shade branches with blood red. Keep the heavy side of the brush toward outside of branch.

Second Background (Optional)

Mix blood-red, shading green.

Shade around main clump with blood red, over ivory.

Shade outer edge of bowl and/or base of cup with shading green, over apple green.

Blend. Avoid padding if possible. Add metallic trim, if desired, following the special instructions in Chapter 3.

Dry and fire.

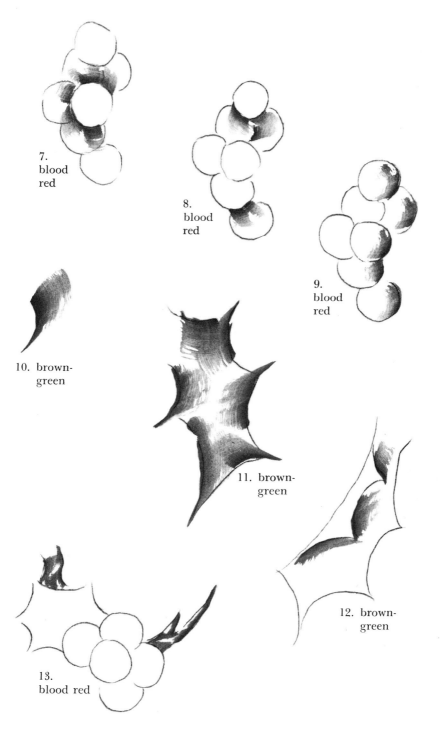

7.
blood
red

8.
blood
red

9.
blood
red

10. brown-
green

11. brown-
green

12. brown-
green

13.
blood red

Fig. 35

Third Coat

Trace in shadows from onionskin using graphite paper. Mix brown-green, shading green, blood red.

STEP 14 — With #8 brush, darken berry divisions, if needed, with blood-red.

STEP 15 — With #8 brush, using comma stroke, shade base of leaves and add centers with shading green.

STEP 16 — Using #8 brush and C stroke, add berry shadows with brown-green. Work from top to bottom.

STEP 17 — With #8 brush, using comma stroke, lightly add shadow leaves with brown-green.

Add second coat of metallic trim, if desired, following the special instructions. Dry and fire.

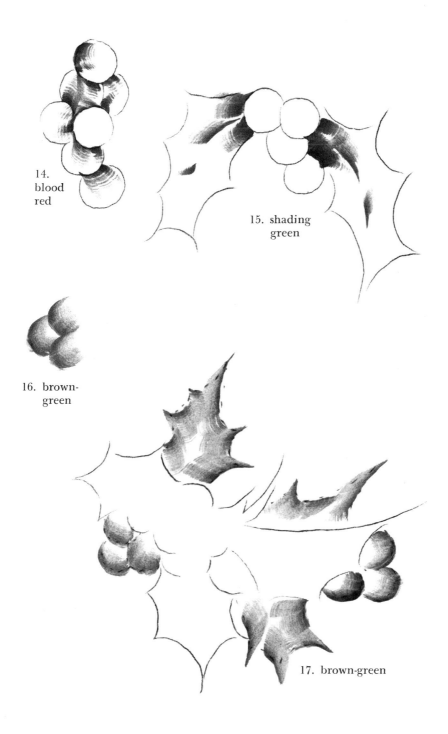

14.
blood
red

15. shading
green

16. brown-
green

17. brown-green

Fig. 36

13

Flowering Dogwood Design

(COLOR PLATES VIII, IX; FIGURES 37-44)

a — Completely outlined flower
b — Incomplete flowers
c — Incomplete leaves
d — Isolated flower
e — Isolated leaves
f — Stems
g — Shadows

Figures 37, 38

STEPS 1, 2 — Trace the designs from the text onto onionskin paper, fit them together as indicated, make a single tracing and transfer to china piece with graphite paper. Do not add shadows on the first coat.

Fig. 37

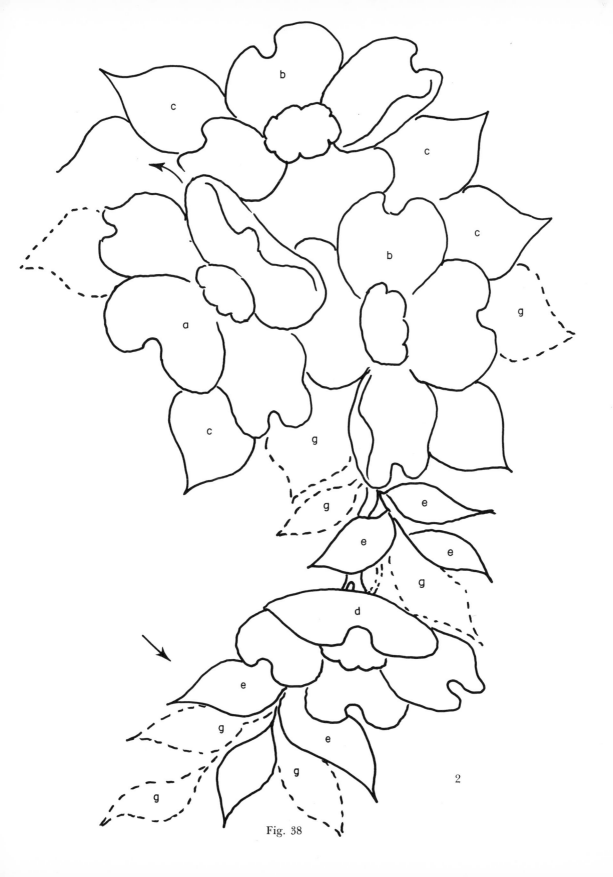

Fig. 38

First Coat

Mix apple green, yellow-green, blue-green, dark yellow and light gray. After gray is mixed, add a little yellow to gray, to give a greenish tinge.

STEP 3 — With #10 brush or ½-inch lettering brush, fill in complete centers of all flowers with yellow. No shading is necessary.

STEP 4 — Spread #10 brush well. Using broken stroke, make halo around centers with yellow-green. Rotate piece as you work. Using C stroke, shade base of each center with yellow-green, over the wet yellow.

STEP 5 — With ½-inch lettering brush, make partial halo around center of isolated flower and shade base of center with yellow-green over the wet yellow.

STEP 6 — With ½-inch brush, lightly outline complete flower with green-gray, which separates the partial flowers but not the petals. Keep heavy side of brush on outline of flower. If too much color has been applied, roll finger very lightly over paint to remove excess.

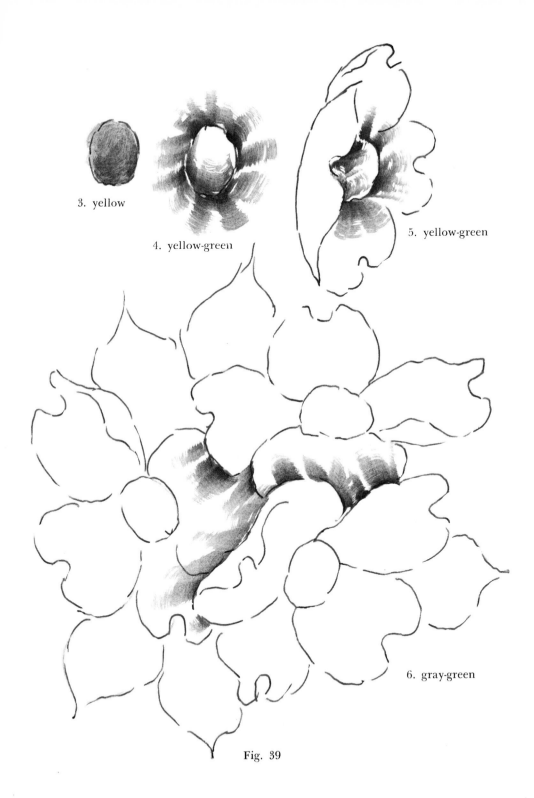

3. yellow

4. yellow-green

5. yellow-green

6. gray-green

Fig. 39

STEP 7 — With ½-inch lettering brush, using a broken stroke, mark the upturned petal, on each side of the yellow center, with gray-green. Fill in all small leaves with yellow tips and apple green at the bases. Blend where the colors meet.

STEP 8 — With #10 brush, fill top of some large leaves and center of other large leaves with yellow.

STEP 9 — With #10 brush, using a broken stroke, partially outline contour of leaves with apple green. Repeat on three or five of the leaves. Outline in same manner on five or seven other leaves with blue-green. This must be done while the yellow is still wet. Blend where the colors meet. Make sure there are no white spots. Refer to the color plate.

STEP 10 — With the side of #10 brush and a broken stroke, fill in stems with yellow-green.

Background and First Firing

Mix light yellow and light blue-green. With ½-inch brush, apply background as already explained. Refer to color plate. Dry and fire first coat.

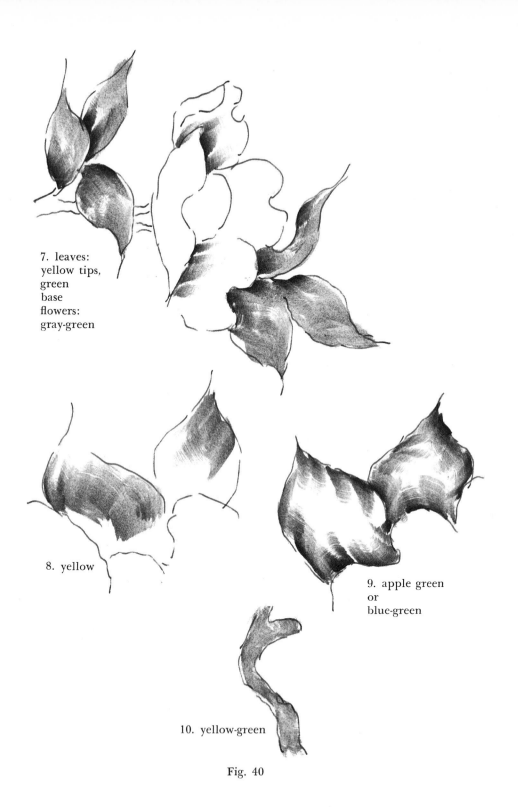

7. leaves:
yellow tips,
green
base
flowers:
gray-green

8. yellow

9. apple green
or
blue-green

10. yellow-green

Fig. 40

Second Coat

Retrace design on piece but do not include the shadows. Mix blood red, dark yellow, add a little yellow to gray to make a gray-green.

STEP 11 (This is a practice figure.) — With #4 brush, using C strokes and comma strokes, practice making small complete circles on your tile.

STEP 12 — With #4 brush, starting at the top of each center, fill centers with these circles with brown-green. Overlap circles as you work.

STEP 13 — With #4 brush, fill center of isolated flower with brown-green.

STEP 14 — With #8 brush, darken separations between flowers with gray-green. Using long broken S stroke, shade under each turned petal.

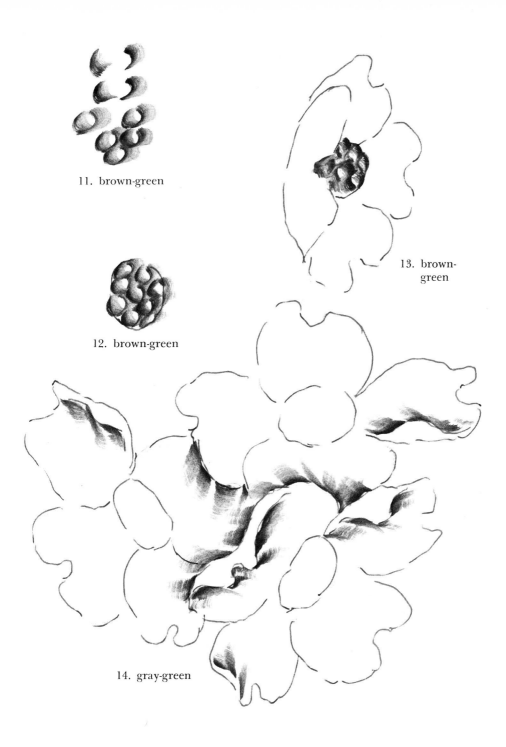

11. brown-green

12. brown-green

13. brown-green

14. gray-green

Fig. 41

STEP 15 — With #8 brush, using long comma strokes, lightly separate petals on each flower and vein with gray-green.

STEP 16 — With #8 brush, separate petals and put in vein on isolated flower with gray-green.

STEP 17 — With #8 brush, using a small broken comma stroke, tip each indentation with blood red.

STEP 18 — With ½-inch brush, outline base of all large leaves where they sit underneath flowers, with brown-green. Keep the heavy side of the brush toward the flower. Make broken comma stroke down center of leaves with brown-green.

110

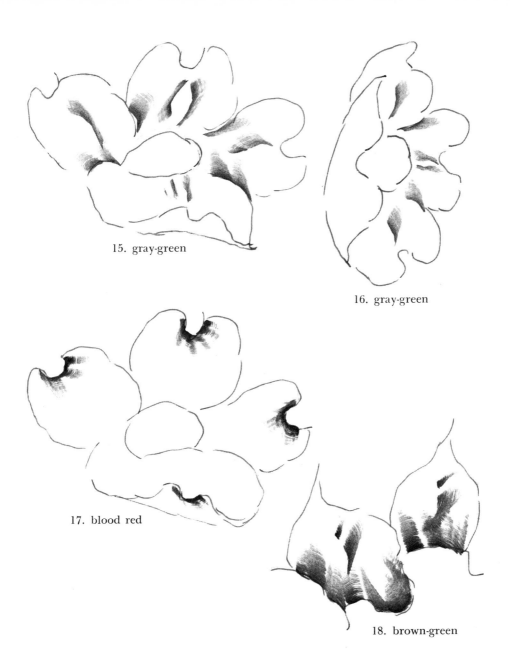

15. gray-green

16. gray-green

17. blood red

18. brown-green

Fig. 42

STEP 19 — With ½-inch brush, lightly shade left side of leaves with brown-green (turn piece so tip of leaf points down). Make comma stroke on leaf tips with brown-green.

STEP 20 — With #8 brush, outline around flower at base of small leaves with brown-green.

STEP 21—With #8 brush, using broken S stroke, tip each small leaf with blood red (turn piece so leaf tip points down). Cut in from the edge on some leaves to give the effect of an upturned leaf.

STEP 22 — With side of #8 brush, lightly stroke in stems with brown-green.

STEP 23 — With #8 brush, shade the stems using blood red over the wet brown-green. Keep the heavy side of the brush to the outer edge of stems so that the blood red is applied only at edges.

Second Background (Optional)

MIX blood red, dark green, and blue-green. Put light yellow over yellow, blue-green over blue-green, and blend the colors where they join.

Refer to color plate. Shade blood red over wet yellow. Dark green is shaded over wet blue-green.

Do not pad. A choppy effect is desirable.

Gold or other metallic trim may be added following the special instructions.

Dry and fire second coat.

112

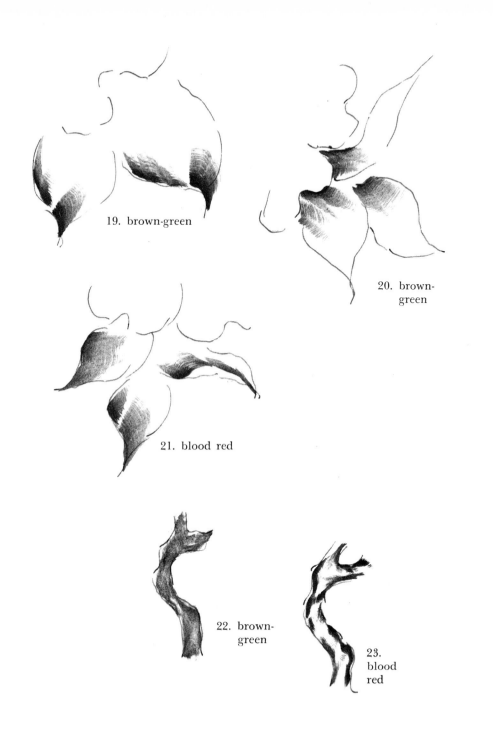

19. brown-green

20. brown-green

21. blood red

22. brown-green

23. blood red

Fig. 43

Third Coat

Mix brown-green, blood red, a pure gray to which a little blood red has been added. This gray mixture is the shadow color. Trace in shadows from onionskin, using graphite paper.

STEP 24 — With #8 brush, using comma stroke, intensify petal tips with blood red. With #8 brush, using comma stroke, put in shadow under centers as shown, with brown-green. With ½-inch of metallic trim, if desired, following the special instructions. Dry brush, using broken S stroke, paint in shadows (dotted on the diagram) with the gray and blood red mixture. Apply second coat and fire.

Color Variation

First coat	Leaves—same; cover all petals pale pink; separate flowers with pink-gray
Background	Pale yellow, baby blue, pale pink
Second coat	Separate petals with a rose-gray mixture. Indentations on the petals should be brown-green or brown
Background	Dark green over baby blue
	Lemon yellow over pale yellow
Shadows	Rose-gray mixture

114

brown-green
at centers

blood red
on tips

gray-red
shadow
mixture

24

Fig. 44

14

Birds and Pine Cones Design

(Color Plates X, XI; Figures 45-51)

Figures 45, 46

Steps 1, 2 — Trace the designs from the text onto onionskin paper, fit them together, make a single tracing and transfer to china piece with graphite paper. You will note that the designs will match and fit a large chop plate.

117

overlap

1

Fig. 45

2

Fig. 46

First Coat

Mix palest yellow, palest blue, blood red, yellow-brown, apple green. Use #8 brush unless otherwise specified.

STEP 3 — Fill in all birds except breasts and beaks with pale blue. Apply thinly.

STEP 4 — Fill in beaks and breasts of all birds with palest yellow.

STEP 5 — While yellow on breasts of bluebirds is still wet, shade very lightly over breasts with blood red.

STEP 6 — Shade lightly on legs and claws of all birds with yellow-brown.

STEP 7 — Completely fill in pine cones with yellow-brown. Partially fill in branches with yellow-brown as shown.

STEP 8 — Using long needle strokes, put in clumps of pine needles with apple green. The base of each clump should be in the un-painted breaks along each branch. *Before applying background, fire.* (It is too difficult to apply background colors between pine needles unless the needle painting has been fired.)

Background

Mix pale yellow, pale pure blue, apple green. Use ½-inch brush. Apply background as in the color plate. Put yellow in the red area at base of stems. The red and the dark green at the base of the stems will be applied later. It is necessary to put apple green fairly dark in the areas between the birds where the pine needles are the thickest. Blend and pad. Dry and fire.

120

3.
pale blue

4.
pale
yellow

5. blood
red

6.
yellow-brown

7.
yellow-
brown

8.
apple green

Fig. 47

Second Coat

Retrace design on piece. Mix brown, any pure blue, brown-green, black. Use #8 brush.

STEP 9 — Shade legs very lightly with brown. Keep heavy side of the brush to the top edge. Put small C stroke on claws with brown.

STEP 10 — Practice making a pointed comma stroke on your tile.

STEP 11 — Using the above stroke, accent the sections of the pine cones with brown. Keep the section points irregular in pattern. It is better if you can do these without tracing.

STEP 12 — Turn pine cones so tips are to your left. Using small C stroke, put centers in each section with brown.

STEP 13 — Using long comma stroke, separate cones with brown where they overlap.

STEP 14 — With a broken stroke, shade all branches with brown. Keep heavy side of brush to the outside of branch.

STEP 15 — Using small comma stroke, shade crotch of branches with brown.

122

9.

10.

11.

12.

13.

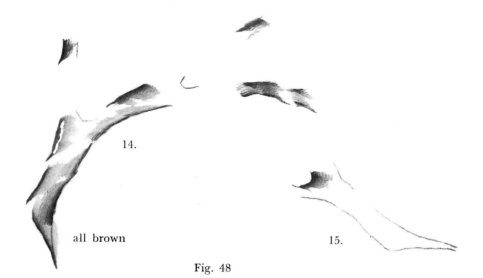

14.

all brown

15.

Fig. 48

STEP 16 — Using a #8 brush and a broken stroke, shade brush and outline around each bird with pure blue. Keep breasts and beaks free of color. Keep heavy side of brush to the outside edge of the bird. Be sure to keep the eye locations free of color. If any color gets in these areas, wipe it off.

STEP 17 — With #4 brush well spread, fill top half of the blue jay's beak lightly with black. Make one line across the bottom of beak with black.

STEP 18 — With #4 brush, lightly shade both beaks of blue birds with black.

STEP 19 — With #8 brush, lightly shade lower edge of blue jay's breast with blue.

STEP 20 — With edge of #8 brush, put in needle clumps with brown-green over first coat. Keep needles in clumps and be sure needle points do not pierce birds. It is necessary to have color fairly solid in the areas between birds.

Second Background

Mix pale yellow, brown-green, violet of iron, apple green, pure blue. Use ½-inch brush. Darken yellow and blue as needed. Apply apple green to base of plate. While it is still wet, apply brown-green over it, as shown in color plate. While yellow is still wet, apply violet of iron over it at the base of branches. Apply halo of yellow-red around bird's head, as in color plate. Blend. Do not pad. A rough effect is desirable. Metallic trim may be added at this time following special instructions in Chapter 3. Dry and fire.

124

16. blue

17. black

18. black

19. black

20.
brown-green

Fig. 49

Third Coat

Mix black, shading green, blood-red.

STEP 21 — With #4 well spread brush, using comma stroke, shade back of eye on blue jay with black.

STEP 22 — Turn plate around. With #4 brush, using small C stroke, shade inside of blue jay's eye with black. Using comma stroke, shade front of eye with black.

STEP 23 — With #8 brush, using broken stroke, shade down back and tip of tail with black. Keep heavy side of brush toward outside edge. Turn plate around. Lightly shade outer edge of breast and add three or four light strokes on the breast. These strokes should be made with the head of the bird down.

STEP 24 — Using #8 brush and broken C stroke, feather in crest and shade around head of blue jay with black. Using broken comma stroke, shade around neck areas with black. Outline head.

STEP 25 — Using #8 brush, broken comma stroke, fill in area between the eye and the crest with black.

STEP 26 — Using #8 brush, a long broken stroke, make a line down center of tail with black.

STEP 27 — With #8 brush, practice on your tile making a sharp pointed comma stroke.

STEP 28 — Using #8 brush and above stroke, mark back and tail of blue jay black.

21.

22.

24.

23.

25.

26.

27.

28.

all black

Fig. 50

STEP 29 — With #4 brush well spread, shade back of eye on sitting bluebird with black.

STEP 30 — With #4 brush, shade front of eye with black. With OO pointer, fill in centers with black. With #8 brush, shade top of head lightly with black.

STEP 31 — With #8 brush, using a broken stroke, feather in lower wing feathers lightly with black. With a straight stroke, shade tail feathers and front edge of bird's body lightly with black.

STEP 32 — With #8 brush, shade breast of bluebirds with blood red. With a straight stroke, make three or four light feather marks with blood red.

STEP 33 — With #8 brush, using small C stroke, put in center of eye on the flying bird with black. Using small comma stroke, put in back of eye on the flying bird with black. Darken bills of both birds if necessary with black. Be sure to have a peaked effect on the beaks.

STEP 34 — With #8 brush, shade around head of flying bird lightly with black. Shade down body and feather in lower wing tips with black. With a broken stroke, feather in tail with black.

STEP 35 — With a #8 brush, lightly tip spread wing feathers of flying bird with black. Using a straight stroke, lightly paint in feather divisions with black. Shade across wing, where it connects to the body, with black.

STEP 36 — With #8 brush, divide the pine cones with yellow-brown.

Background

Darken base of plate if needed. Add second coat of metallic trim, if desired, following special instructions. Dry and fire.

128

29. black

30. black

31. black

32. blood red

33. black

34. black

35. black

36. brown

Fig. 51

15

Full-Bloom Rose Design

(Color Plates XII, XIII; Figures 52-60)

a — Full bloom rose
b — Large bud
c — Turned flower
d — Bud
e — Isolated leaves
f — Partial leaves under flowers
g — Stems
h — Shadows

Figures 52, 53

Steps 1, 2 — This is the master drawing for a cake plate or a large chop platter. Trace the designs, including stems, onto onionskin paper. Do not trace in shadows. Fit the two pages together after tracing and transfer the design directly on to the platter. You may trace from the color plate for an eight-inch plate or smaller piece such as butter dish.

131

overlap

Fig. 52

Fig. 53

First Coat

Mix pale yellow, pale pink, lemon yellow, apple green, blue-green, pale yellow. Use #10 or ¾-inch ferrule type brush.

STEP 3 — Coat full bloom rose with pale yellow. Using C stroke, while yellow is still wet, mark left side of bowl of rose with pale pink. Using C stroke, mark inside of bottom of bowl with pale pink. Using broken comma stroke, outline right side of bowl with pink. Using broken stroke, outline edge of petals as shown with pink.

STEP 4 — Coat bud center with pale yellow. Shade base of center with pink.

STEP 5 — Lightly coat large bud with pale yellow. Using C stroke while yellow is still wet, mark bottom and left side of bowl with pink. Using broken comma stroke, outline top and right side of bowl with pink. Using broken stroke, outline edge of all petals with pink. Using corner stroke, mark center with pink.

STEP 6 — Lightly coat turned flower with pale yellow. Using C stroke while yellow is still wet, mark bowl. Mark petals with pink using straight stroke. Using broken corner stroke, mark divisions where flowers overlap with pink.

134

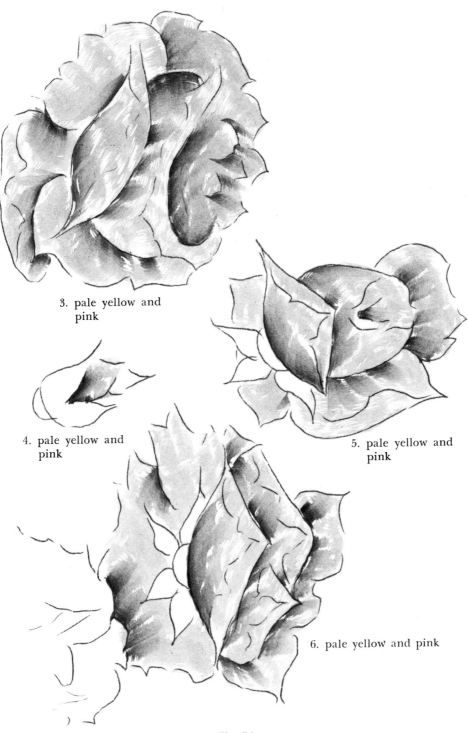

3. pale yellow and
   pink

4. pale yellow and
   pink

5. pale yellow and
   pink

6. pale yellow and pink

Fig. 54

STEP 7 — Shade isolated leaves with lemon yellow. Refer to color plate and note how sunshine sifts through on the left side of the design.

STEP 8 — Shade in shadow side of isolated leaves with apple green. Leaves should be completely covered with color. Blend where color overlaps to eliminate any sharp line.

STEP 9 — Shade tips of partial leaves with lemon yellow.

STEP 10 — Shade base of partial leaves where they appear under flowers with apple green. Using broken stroke while green is still wet, shade same area with blue-green.

STEP 11 — Fill in flower calyxes with apple green.

STEP 12 — Fill in bud calyx with apple green.

STEP 13 — Lightly fill in stems with apple green.

Background and First Firing

Mix pale yellow, light blue, apple green. With ½-inch brush, apply background as already explained. See color plate. (Dark green and violet of iron will be added later.) Blend and pad. Dry and fire.

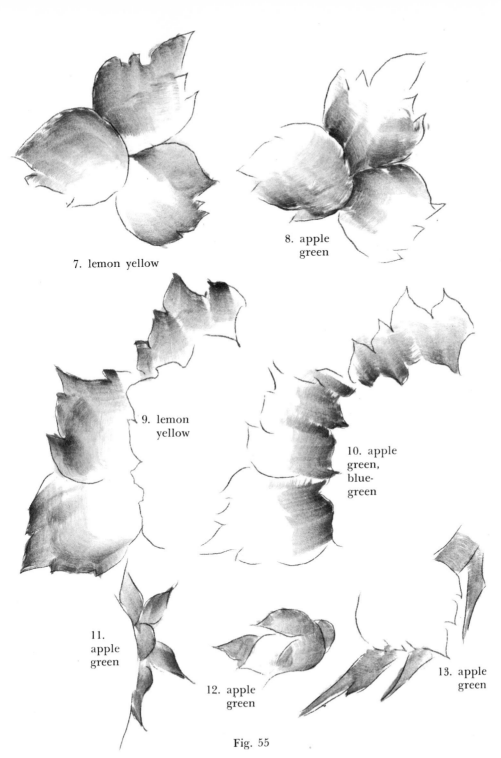

7. lemon yellow

8. apple green

9. lemon yellow

10. apple green, blue-green

11. apple green

12. apple green

13. apple green

Fig. 55

Second Coat

Retrace design on piece. Do not trace in shadows. Mix pale pink, apple green, brown-green, any true rose. Divide pink into two parts. Add a little apple green to one portion to make pinky gray.

Use #8 brush. Intensify on full bloom rose with light pink as needed. Intensify buds and turned flower with rose as shown in Steps 3 through 6.

STEP 14 — Using a broken stroke, outline where each petal turns with pinky gray.

STEP 15 — Mark center of full bloom rose with rose.

STEP 16 — Using comma stroke, mark tip of small bud and intensify base of bud with rose.

STEP 17 — Divide rose into two portions. Mix apple green into one portion to make a rose-gray.
Using a broken stroke, outline all turned petals of large bud with rose-gray. Using a comma stroke, mark center of large bud with pure rose.

STEP 18 — With broken strokes mark turned petals on turned flower with rose-gray. Darken shading where flowers overlap with rose-gray.

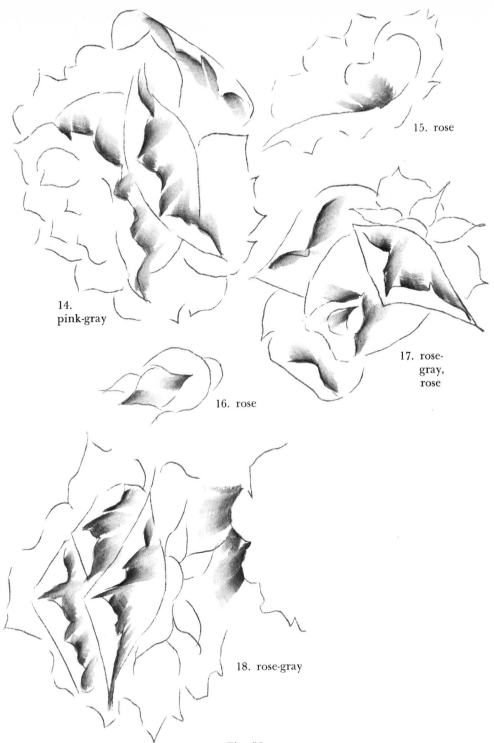

14.
pink-gray

15. rose

17. rose-
gray,
rose

16. rose

18. rose-gray

Fig. 56

STEP 19 — Outline base of whole leaf in isolated leaf clump with brown-green. Rotate plate as you work. Using broken comma strokes, put in centers of leaves with brown-green. Stroke toward the tip of leaf. Do not put any color on the actual tips of the leaves.

STEP 20 — With #10 brush, using broken strokes, shade all partial leaves where they appear under flowers with brown-green. Keep heavy side of brush toward flower. Blend color lines with finger so there is no harsh line.

STEP 21 — With #10 brush and using broken comma strokes, separate leaves where they overlap with brown-green.

STEP 22 — With #8 brush, using small C stroke, shade base of small bud calyx with brown-green. With larger C stroke, shade bowl of small bud calyx with brown-green.

STEP 23 — Turn plate so calyx points down. Using S stroke, shade tips of calyx with brown-green.

STEP 24 — Using small C stroke, shade bases of flower calyxes with brown-green.

STEP 25 — Using S stroke, shade fingers of calyxes with brown-green. Rotate plate as you paint.

STEP 26 — Using broken straight stroke, shade all edges of stems with brown-green. Keep heavy side of brush toward outside of stems.

Second Background (Optional)

Using ½-inch brush, darken pale yellow and blue where needed. Shade around stems with dark green at base of plate. While green is still wet, shade over base areas with violet of iron as in color plate. Metallic trim may be added, following the special instructions in Chapter 3. Dry and fire.

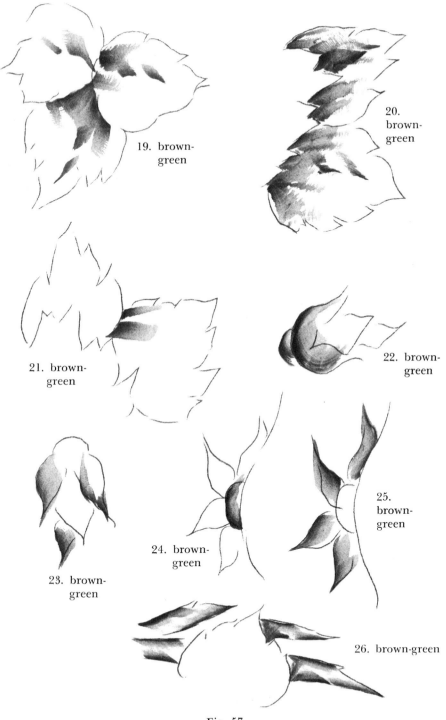

19. brown-green

20. brown-green

21. brown-green

22. brown-green

23. brown-green

24. brown-green

25. brown-green

26. brown-green

Fig. 57

Third Coat

Trace in shadows from onionskin, using graphite paper. Mix violet of iron, ruby or maroon, dark green. Divide ruby into two portions. Add dark green to make ruby-gray. Use #8 brush

STEP 27 — Separate lower petals with ruby-gray.

STEP 28 — Using the edge of brush and comma stroke, put in center of full bloom rose with pure ruby.

STEP 29 — Shade all turned petals on large bud with ruby-gray. Put S stroke on outer petals with ruby-gray. Separate outer petals with ruby-gray.

STEP 30 — With #8 brush shade bowl and outline top edge of petals with pure ruby.

STEP 31 — Using S stroke, stroke through center of small bud with pure ruby.

STEP 32 — Shade base of large bud and top edge of petals with pure ruby. Using C stroke, shade left side of bowl with pure ruby. Using broken comma stroke, shade outer side of right side of bowl with pure ruby. Make three little comma strokes in center of large bud with pure ruby.

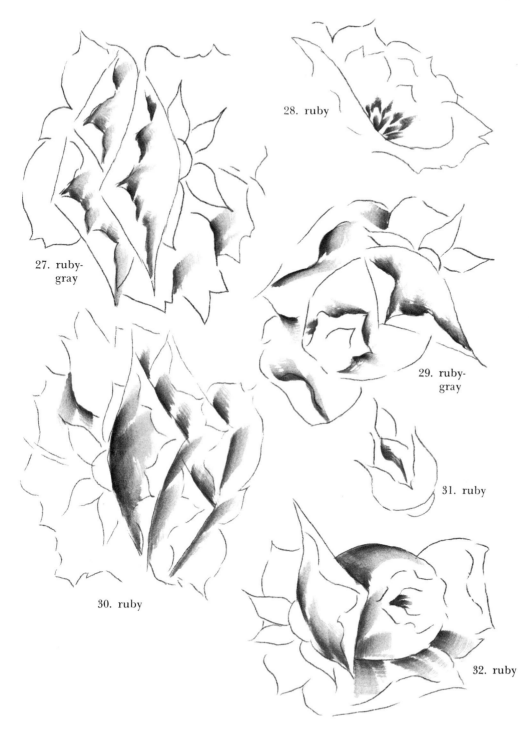

27. ruby-
gray

28. ruby

29. ruby-
gray

30. ruby

31. ruby

32. ruby

Fig. 58

STEP 33 — With #10 brush, using broken stroke, darken base of leaves where needed with dark green, particularly at base of flower clump.

STEP 34 — With #8 brush, using broken comma stroke, make jagged effect on leaf tips with violet of iron. Keep heavy side of brush to outside of leaves.

STEP 35 — Outline edge of heavy stems with violet of iron. Keep heavy side of brush to the outside of stems. Darken where stems go under leaves with violet of iron.

STEP 36 — Using edge of #8 brush and small sharp comma strokes, add thorns to heavy stems with violet of iron.

STEP 37 — Using edge of #8 brush, outline top of thin stems and add thorns with violet of iron.

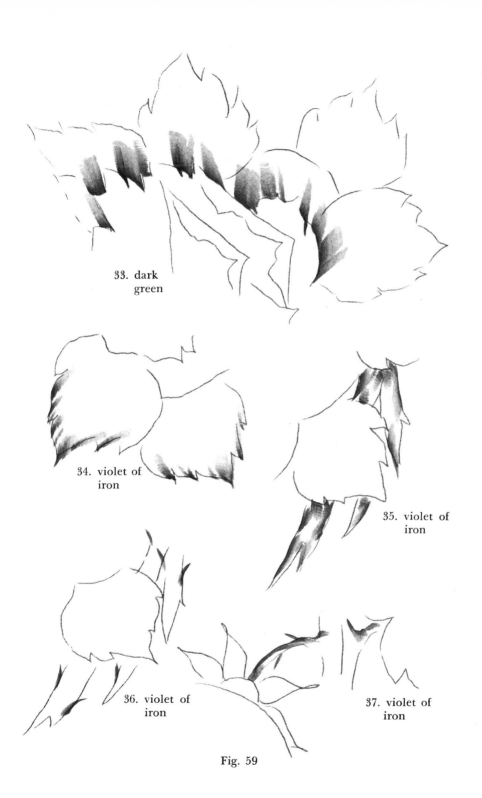

33. dark
green

34. violet of
iron

35. violet of
iron

36. violet of
iron

37. violet of
iron

Fig. 59

STEP 38 — Using #10 brush or ½-inch brush, well spread, make long broken S stroke down left side of isolated shadow leaves with violet of iron. Keep shadows very light. Turn plate around and make long S stroke down opposite side.

STEP 39 — Using broken stroke, shade base of all shadow leaves with violet of iron.

STEP 40 — Using broken S stroke, shade tips of shadow leaves, violet of iron.

STEP 41 — Using small C stroke, shade base of calyx with violet of iron.

STEP 42 — Using large C stroke, shade bowl of calyx with violet of iron. With S stroke put in center of bud with violet of iron.

STEP 43 — With S stroke, put in finger petals of bud with violet of iron.

STEP 44 — Using side of #10 brush, and broken stroke, put in stems with violet of iron. Finished shadow bud should appear as shown.

Add second application of metallic trim, if desired, following the special instructions. Dry and fire.

Color Variation

First coat	Coat rose with yellow
	Shade with yellow-red
Background	Pale yellow, true green
Second coat	Shade rose with yellow-brown
	Add highlights with lemon yellow
Background	Shading green, yellow-red accent
Third coat	Brown-green shadows

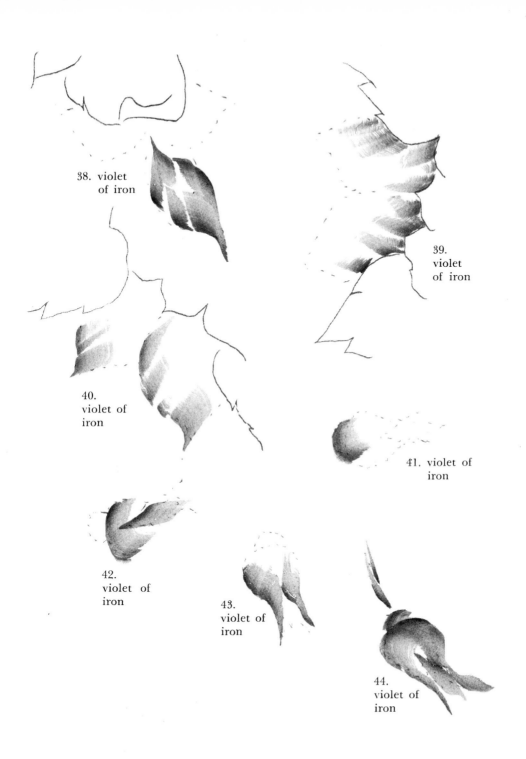

38. violet
of iron

39.
violet
of iron

40.
violet of
iron

41. violet of
iron

42.
violet of
iron

43.
violet of
iron

44.
violet of
iron

Fig. 60

The Bluebird and Blue Jay Design with Pine Cones

(COLOR PLATES X AND XI)

Birds are one of the most popular and interesting designs in china painting. The shading as shown in this text can be used as a basic system for doing other varieties of birds. Using the same shading instructions, substitute the other colors which identify the bird you wish to paint. Be careful to note the eyes and expression of the bird.

You may use any part of this design rather than the whole. One bird alone can be effective on china, or, you may wish to use only parts of the branches. If you wish to reverse the design or any portion of it, trace the pattern onto tracing paper and then turn the paper over.

This design is very striking. It makes a beautiful wall decoration on plaques or plates. Birds done on large tankards are effective. When doing a tankard, reverse the design and place the blue jay next to the handle. Pitchers should be done in the same manner. Large flower vases and lamps take this design well.

First
coat

Second
coat

X. Birds and Pine Cones

Third
coat

XI.   Birds and Pine Cones for a Chop Plate

The Pink Full-Bloom Rose Design

(Color Plates XII and XIII)

The rose is one of the most beautiful of all flowers. It is the national flower of England and the official flower of Georgia, New York, District of Columbia, Iowa and North Dakota. There are thousands of different varieties of roses which come in a wide range of colors but never in blue.

The rose design may be applied to most any piece. Tea and coffee sets, full sets of dinnerware, platters and decorative pieces, large flower vases or rose jars will all take this design effectively. It is one of the most commonly used in china painting.

Colors as shown in the color plate

First coat	Flowers, buds — pale pink, pale yellow, apple green
	Leaves — Lemon yellow, apple green, blue-green
Background	Pale yellow, light blue, apple green
Second coat	Flowers, buds — pink-gray, rose, rose-gray, brown-green
	Leaves — brown-green
Background	Pale yellow, blue, violet of iron
Third coat	Flowers, buds — ruby-gray, pure ruby
	Leaves — dark green
	Stems — violet of iron
Shadows	Violet of iron

First
coat

Second
coat

XII.   Full-Bloom Rose Design

XIII.   Full-Bloom Rose on a Cake Plate

The Black Cherry Design

The black cherry is a small round fruit which makes a delightful and informal design for painting. It should be put on casual pieces such as fruit bowls and cookie jars. Flower vases and condiment sets used on the breakfast table are attractive with this design. Egg dishes, cereal bowls and all sizes of mugs are pretty with cherries on them. Hot chocolate pots with matching cups and saucers make an unusual breakfast setting. Cherries are also lovely for larger tankards and the large jugs.

Colors as shown in color plate

First coat	Cherries — pale yellow shaded with ruby
	Leaves — lemon yellow and chartreuse
Background	Pale yellow, baby blue
Second coat	Cherries — shade with purple
	Leaves — Brown-green
	Branches — violet of iron
Background	Accent with blood red over yellow
	Purple over blue at base
Third coat	Cherries — shaded with purple and dark green mixture
Shadows	Purple and blood red mixture

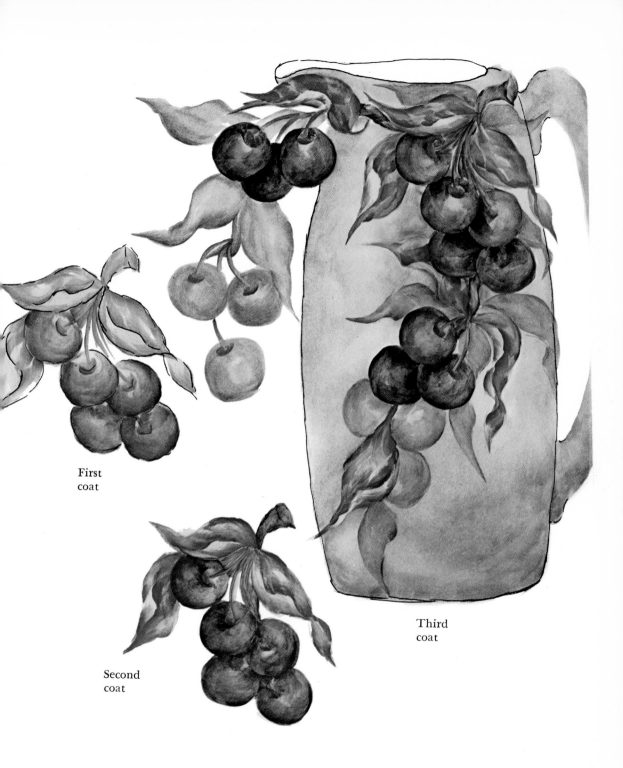

First
coat

Second
coat

Third
coat

XIV. Black Cherries on a Hot Chocolate Jug

The Baby White Rose Design

Color Plate XV

The baby white rose is a small, delicate design and one of the most commonly used flowers in china painting. It is very appropriate for putting on dresserware, jewelry, pin boxes, powder boxes, and also dinnerware. Candlesticks painted with the baby rose to match the place settings can help make an attractive looking table. This design is slightly more formal than the other flowers.

Colors in color plate

First coat	Flower — shade with gray, yellow-green; yellow centers
	Leaves — lemon yellow, apple green
Background	Light yellow, light Russian- or blue-green at base
Second coat	Flowers — shade with gray, yellow-red in centers
	Leaves — shade base with dark yellow-green or chartreuse
	Buds — small touch of yellow-red in center
Background	Yellow-red over pale yellow, darken with blue-green if desired
Third coat	Flower — gray if needed
	Leaves — brown-green and blood red tips
	Shadows — gray

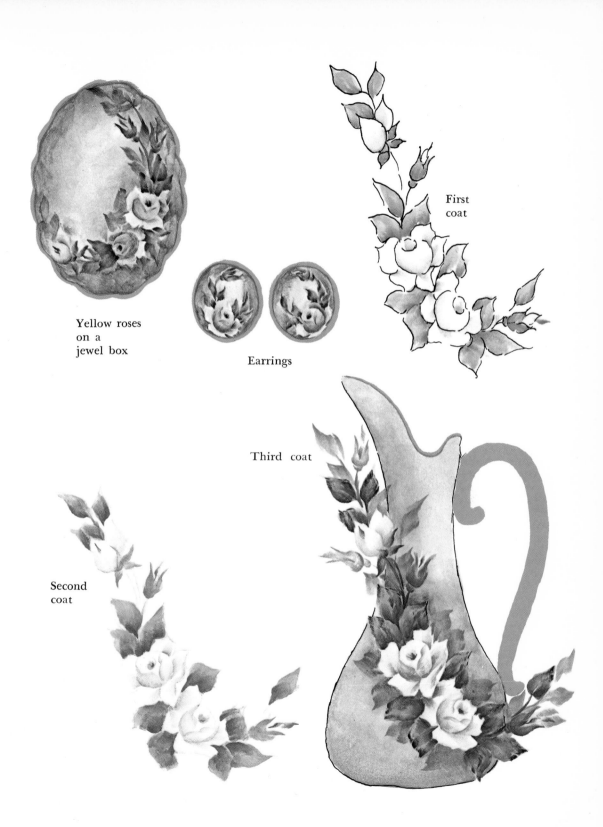

Yellow roses
on a
jewel box

Earrings

First
coat

Second
coat

Third coat

XV.   White Baby Rose Design

The Fern Design

The fern design is a quick and easy pattern which is done in monochrome. It may be done in any color, using three shades of the same color to complete the piece. Ferns may be painted in any size. If background is desired, apply it first and fire before proceeding to trace the design.

Dinnerware is lovely with the fern. Any luncheon or dessert set is appropriate for this design. The fern can be used for formal place settings or on single pieces such as bonbon dishes, trays, and bowls.

The fern design may also be painted attractively with tones of blue, blue-greens or browns. Gray or black fern patterns are effective.

First coat

Second coat

Cup

Salt
and
pepper

XVI. Fern Dinnerware

The Forget-Me-Not Design

The forget-me-not is a small and delicate flower. The plant has light green leaves and slightly fuzzy stems. A forget-me-not is the legendary symbol of friendship and love, and is also the state flower of Alaska.

Small china pieces can be beautifully decorated with this design. Any dresserware, small vases or lamps and jewelry are appropriate for this flower. Earrings and brooches designed with forget-me-nots make sentimental and lovely gifts.

On a large piece forget-me-nots may be scattered in small clumps. Dinnerware is attractive in this design.

Colors shown in color plate

First coat	Flowers — pale blue
	Leaves — medium yellow, apple green
Background	Baby blue, pale yellow
Second coat	Flowers — Any medium blue with yellow red centers
	Leaves — Brown-green
	Buds — Pale blue
Second background	Yellow-red accent over pale yellow
Shadows	Gray with a little blue added

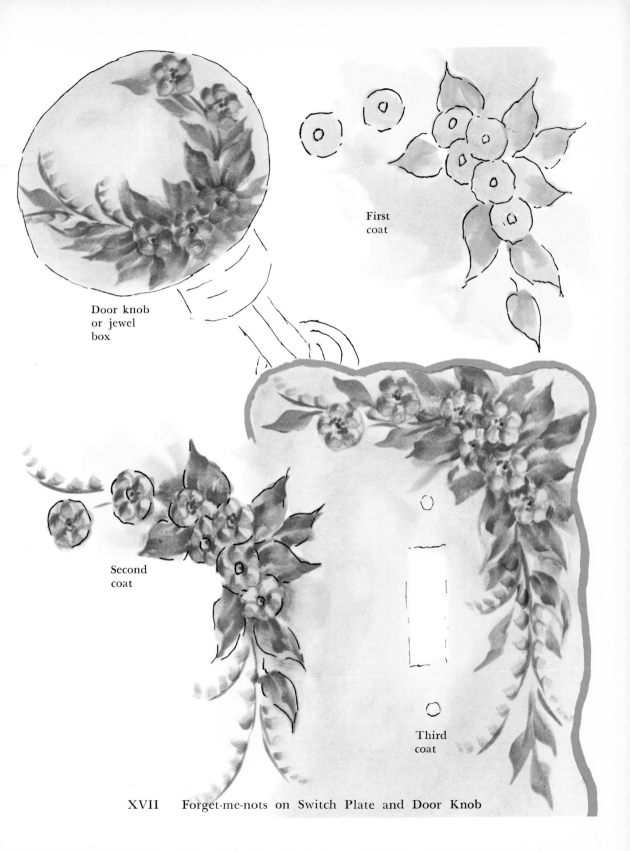

Door knob
or jewel
box

First
coat

Second
coat

Third
coat

XVII   Forget-me-nots on Switch Plate and Door Knob

16

Black Cherry Design

(COLOR PLATE XIV; FIGURES 61-65)

a — Whole cherries
b — Incomplete cherries. Note that these cherries are partially covered
c — Leaves. Note that each of these leaves is partially turned
d — Branches
e — Shadows

Figures 61, 62

STEPS 1, 2 — Trace from this design for chocolate pot or large vase. Do not add shadows. Fit Steps 1 and 2 together to make complete design as in the color plate. If cherries are not round, trace around penny.

Use any part of this design to fit chocolate cups. Trace from the color plate for small vases, jugs, cookie jars or eight-inch plates.

149

overlap

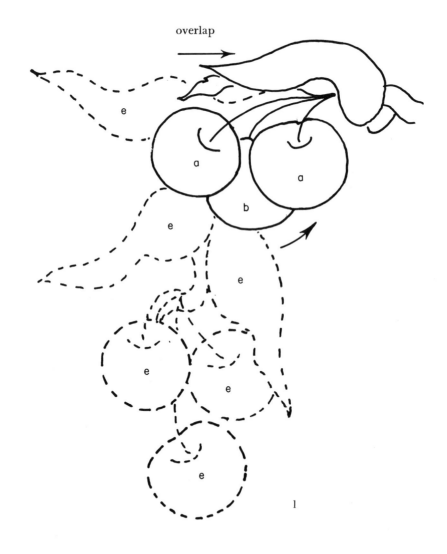

Fig. 61

Fig. 62

First Coat

Mix pale yellow, ruby, lemon yellow, dark yellow-green or chartreuse. Use ½-inch or #10 brush throughout.

STEP 3 — Coat cherries ivory. Do *one* clump at a time and then follow instructions in Steps 4 and 5. Repeat same procedure for remaining clumps.

STEP 4 — Using small C stroke while pale yellow is still wet, put in cherry centers with chartreuse. Using the side of the brush, add stems with chartreuse.

STEP 5 — While pale yellow is still wet, outline each cherry with ruby. Keep heavy side of brush to outside of cherry.

STEP 6 — Coat leaves with lemon yellow. Do two or three at a time, then proceed with instructions in Step 7. Repeat.

STEP 7 — While yellow is still wet, shade under each turned portion of each leaf and around edge with chartreuse. Fill stems with chartreuse.

Backgrounding and First Firing

Mix pale yellow, baby blue.

With ½-inch brush, coat most of area with pale yellow. With ½-inch brush, work in blue at base of handle and jug.

Blend and pad. Dry and fire.

152

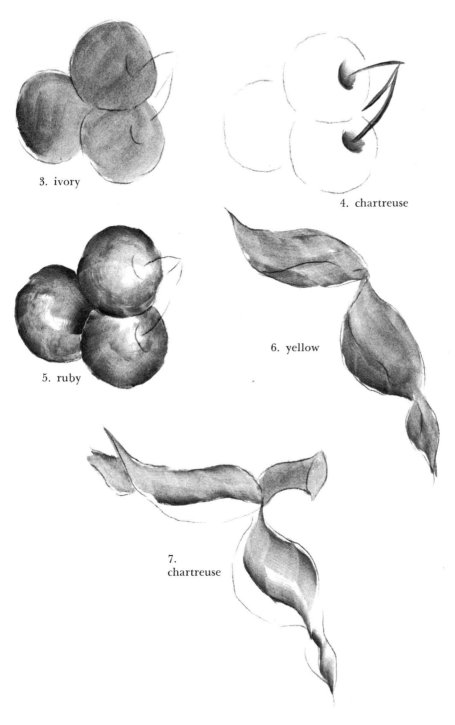

3. ivory

4. chartreuse

5. ruby

6. yellow

7. chartreuse

Fig. 63

Second Coat

Retrace design on piece. Do not trace on shadows. Mix purple, brown-green, violet of iron (mix violet of iron by adding a little purple to blood red).

STEP 8 — Using ½-inch brush well spread, outline underneath each cherry and shade outside edge of each cherry with purple.

STEP 9 — Using #8 brush, with small C stroke, put in centers with brown green.

STEP 10 — Using #8 brush, shade all turned leaves and outline outer edges with brown green.

STEP 11 — With #8 brush, shade branches with violet of iron. Keep heavy side of brush to outside of branch. If first coat is pale, coat stem first with brown-green.

Second Background (Optional)

Using ½-inch brush, intensify first background colors.
Shade around center clump with blood red over the pale yellow.
Shade base of jug with purple over blue as in the color plate.
Blend and pad. Metallic trim may be added, if desired, following the special instructions in Chapter 3. Dry and fire.

154

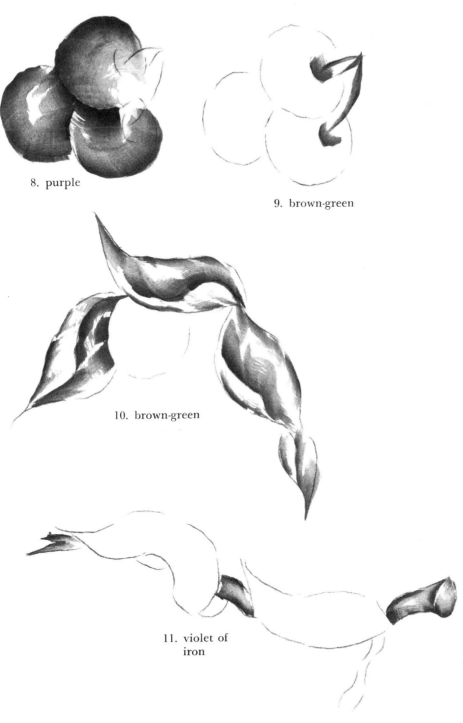

8. purple

9. brown-green

10. brown-green

11. violet of
    iron

Fig. 64

Third Coat

Trace in shadows from onionskin using graphite paper. Mix purple, darkest green; divide purple into two piles. Add darkest green to one pile for shading. Add a little blood red to other pile to make shadow mixture.

STEP 12 — With #8 brush, shade each cherry which lies underneath another with purple to which a little dark green has been added.

STEP 13 — With ½-inch brush, lightly shade with long S stroke on all shadow leaves with shadow color.

STEP 14 — With ½-inch brush, lightly put in shadow cherries with shadow color. With #8 brush, using small C stroke, put in centers of cherries with shadow mixture. With the side of #8 brush, add stems to shadow cherries with shadow color. Darken leaves if necessary.

Add second coat of metallic trim if desired following the special instructions, Chapter 3. Dry and fire.

Color Variation

First coat	Cherries ivory and Persian red, leaves the same
Background	Ivory, apple green
Second coat	Shade cherries blood red, leaves the same
Background	Accent with blood red over ivory, shading green over apple

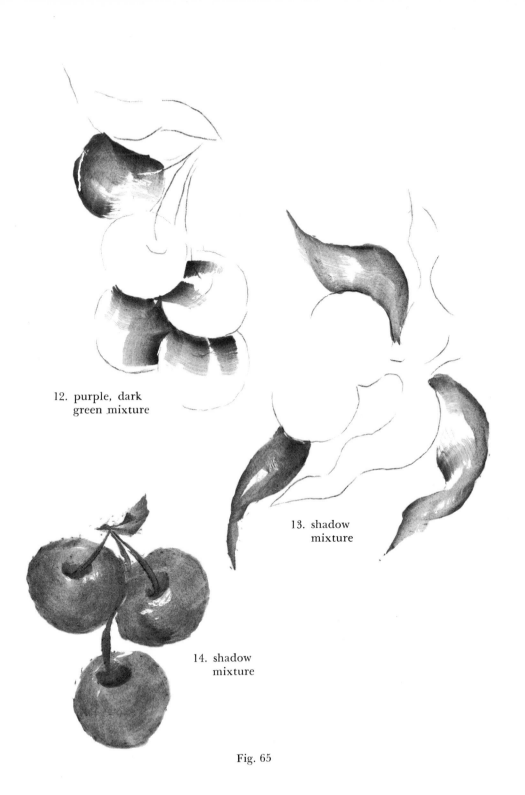

12. purple, dark
    green mixture

13. shadow
    mixture

14. shadow
    mixture

Fig. 65

17

Baby Rose Design

(COLOR PLATE XV; FIGURES 66-71)

a — Complete flower
b — Incomplete flower
c — Isolated flower
d — Buds
e — Leaves
f — Shadow buds
g — Shadow leaves

Figure 66

STEP 1 — This is the master drawing for baby white roses on a small
pitcher vase. Trace the design direct from this illustration. You
may also use this design on a small eight-inch plate or candy dish
by reversing the lower part to follow the curve of the plate.

Refer to the color plate for each coat of color. Remember the
easiest error made on baby roses is the application of too much paint
on the blossoms.

Fig. 66

Figure 67

STEP 2 — Smaller pieces, such as a powder box, take the baby rose design well, and it can easily be adapted to jewelry. A pin and earrings are shown here.

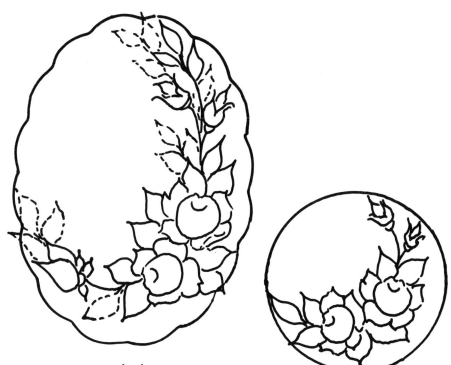

powder box

pin

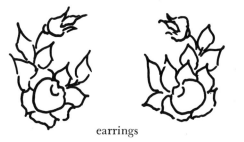

earrings

2

Fig. 67

First Coat

Trace design on to onionskin paper and apply to china with graphite. Do not include shadows or stems. Mix yellow-green, gray, lemon yellow, apple green. Use #6 brush.

STEP 3 — Using broken comma stroke, shade lightly under bowl of flower with yellow-green

STEP 4 — Using C stroke, shade left side of bowl very lightly with gray.

STEP 5 — Using broken comma stroke, shade outer side of right side of bowl with gray. Skip over yellow-green area.

STEP 6 — Outline base of complete flower in order to separate flowers, with gray

STEP 7 — Using C stroke, shade base of isolated flower with gray.

STEP 8 — Using comma stroke, outline outer side of bowl on the isolated flower with gray.

STEP 9 — Turn china so bud points down. Using small comma stroke, tip isolated flower with gray.

STEP 10 — Using small C stroke, shade centers with yellow.

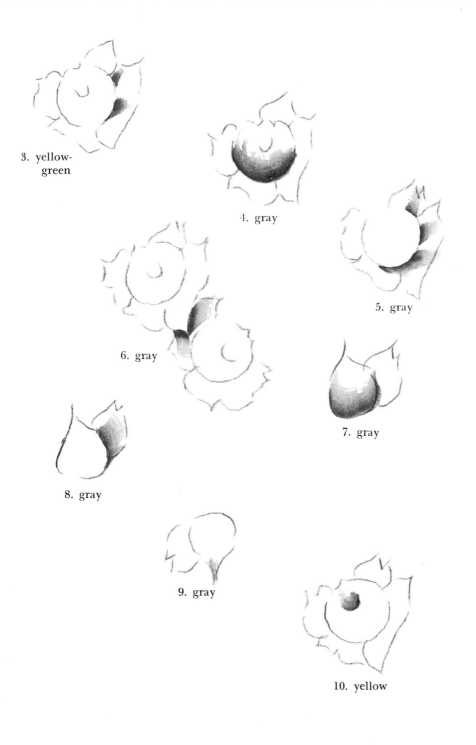

3. yellow-
green

4. gray

5. gray

6. gray

7. gray

8. gray

9. gray

10. yellow

Fig. 68

STEP 11 — Fill all isolated leaves with lemon yellow. No shading is necessary.

STEP 12 — Tip other leaves with yellow.

STEP 13 — Shade base of leaves under flowers with apple green.

STEP 14 — Shade base of small leaves with apple green.

STEP 15 — Using small C stroke, shade calyx of isolated flower with apple green.

STEP 16 — Using small S stroke, shade fingers of calyx with apple green.

STEP 17 — Using small C stroke, shade base of bud with apple green.

STEP 18 — Using large C stroke, shade bowl of bud with apple green.

STEP 19 — Turn so bud tip points down. Make two small S strokes on calyx. Complete calyx must be covered with apple green.

Background and First Firing

Use 1/2-inch brush apply background as already explained. Shade light yellow to the top of piece. Shade light Russian or blue-green around flowers and at base. Blend and pad. Dry and fire first coat.

164

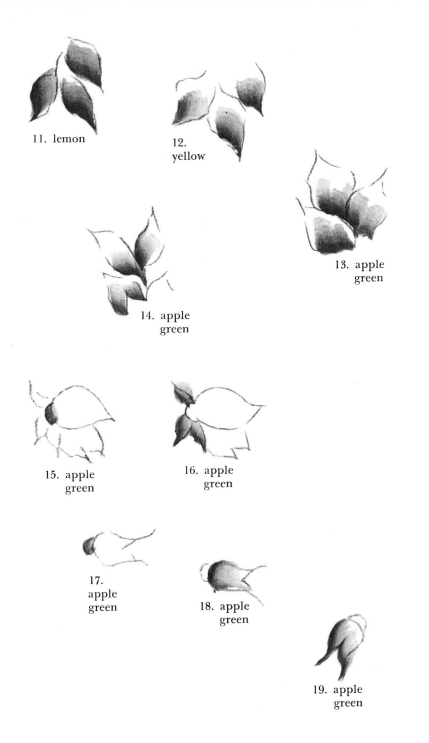

11. lemon

12. yellow

13. apple green

14. apple green

15. apple green

16. apple green

17. apple green

18. apple green

19. apple green

Fig. 69

Second Coat

Retrace design on piece. Do not trace on shadows. Use #6 brush. Mix gray, yellow-red, chartreuse.

STEP 20 — Intensify around bowl and inside bowl and between flowers with gray if needed.

STEP 21 — Add yellow-red to center, with three small strokes.

STEP 22 — Using long S stroke, turn bottom petal of complete flower with gray.

STEP 23 — Using long S stroke, shade right side of center with gray.

STEP 24 — Turn piece around and put long S stroke on left side with gray.

STEP 25 — Turn piece so bud points down. With comma stroke, paint through center of isolated flower with yellow-red.

STEP 26 — Using small S stroke, paint down center of each bud with yellow-red.

STEP 27 — Shade base of all large leaves with chartreuse.

STEP 28 — Using S stroke, shade base of all small leaves with chartreuse.

Second Background (Optional)

Darken colors if desired. Apply yellow-red over pale yellow around flowers. Blend. Avoid padding if possible. Metallic trim may be added at this time following special instructions in Chapter 3. Dry and fire.

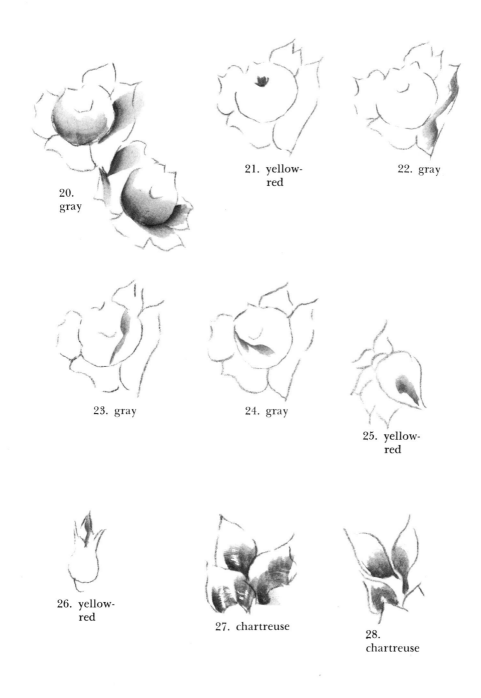

20. gray

21. yellow-red

22. gray

23. gray

24. gray

25. yellow-red

26. yellow-red

27. chartreuse

28. chartreuse

Fig. 70

Third Coat

Trace in shadows from onionskin, using graphite paper. Mix gray, brown-green, blood red.

STEP 29 — Intensify gray on flowers as needed.

STEP 30 — Shade base of all large leaves with brown-green.

STEP 31 — Using small broken comma stroke, make centers in all large leaves with brown-green.

STEP 32 — Shade bud: small C at base, large C in bowl, comma stroke on tips, brown-green.

STEP 33 — Shade base of all small leaves with brown-green.

STEP 34 — Using a broken stroke, shade tips of all large leaves with blood red.

STEP 35 — Using comma stroke, shade tips of small leaves with blood red.

STEP 36 — With the side of the brush, add stems as needed with brown-green.

STEP 37 — Using a long broken S stroke, add shadow leaves with pure gray.

STEP 38 — Using small C stroke, shade base of bud with gray.

STEP 39 — Using large C stroke, shade bowl of bud with gray.

STEP 40 — Using long S stroke, paint through center of bud with gray.

STEP 41 — Turn piece so bud points down. Make two long S strokes on fingers of bud calyx with gray.

STEP 42 — Add shadow stems where needed with gray.

Add second application of metallic trim, if desired, following the special instructions. Dry and fire.

168

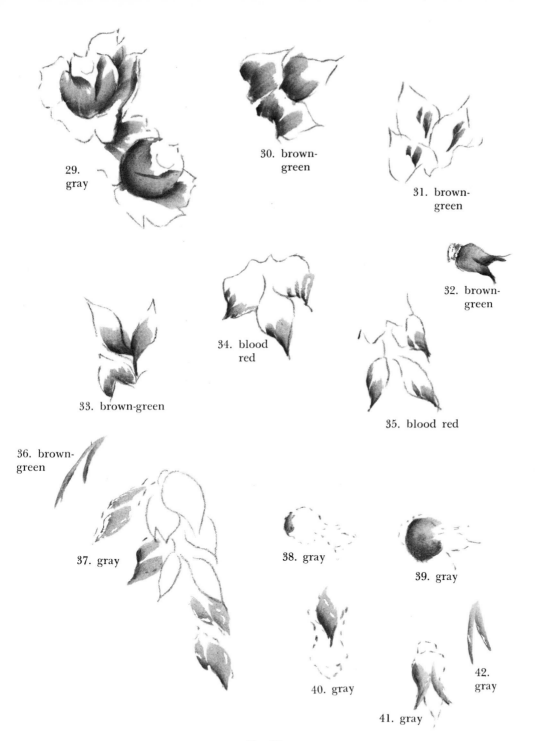

29.
gray

30. brown-
green

31. brown-
green

32. brown-
green

33. brown-green

34. blood
red

35. blood red

36. brown-
green

37. gray

38. gray

39. gray

40. gray

41. gray

42.
gray

Fig. 71

Color Variations

First coat	Coat with ivory.
	Shade bowl with yellow-brown
	Shade leaves with dark blue-green
	Yellow on leaf tips
Background	Ivory, blue-green
Second coat	Shade bowl yellow-red
	Shade center with blood red
	Shade leaves with blood red, brown-green
Background	Shading green
	Blue-green shadows

WHITE WITH RUBY CENTER

First coat	Shade with rose gray
	Pale pink in centers
	Leaves — pale ivory on tips, blue-green on base
Background	Predominantly blue and pink
Second coat	Shade with rose-gray
	Ruby in centers
	Brown-green on leaves, ruby tips
Background	Ruby over pink
	Purple over blue around design and to the base of china upright piece
	Rose-gray shadows

170

PINK

First coat	Coat with ivory
	Shade bowl with pale pink
	Leaves with blue-green. Yellow tips
Background	Ivory, pink, blue
Second coat	Shade with strong pink and pink-gray
	Ruby in centers
	Leaves — blue-green, violet of iron tips
Background	Blue, rose, and ruby
	Rose-gray shadows

RUBY

First coat	Coat with ivory
	Shade bowl with pale pink
	Leaves with blue-green. Yellow tips
Background	Ivory, pink, blue
Second coat	Shade with strong rose and brown-green leaves
Background	Pink, blue, pale yellow
Third coat	Shade flowers with ruby and ruby-gray

SALMON

First coat	Coat with ivory. Use any iron red to shade flower. Test fire the red over ivory first
	Centers with yellow
Background	Pale yellow predominantly, apple green
Second coat	Shade bowl with iron red
	Centers with blood red
	Shade flower with red-gray
Background	Iron red over pale yellow partially
	Shading green over apple
	Tip leaves with blood red

18

Fern Design

(COLOR PLATE XVI; FIGURES 72-76)

Figure 72

STEP 1 — Trace from this drawing. This is a spray with three points. It can be done in any size. The shortest spray should be slightly less than one-half the length of the longest spray.

The medium sized spray should be approximately two-thirds the length of the longest spray.

In placing the design, divide the border into three five or seven equal sections. Make one basic spray and retrace on each section of the border.

This same basic spray may be used with leaves to make attractive dinnerware. In this case, a variety of colors may be used. Keep the first coat of color light, the second coat darker and shade around each spray with background color. The main thing to remember is to keep the brush strokes loose and feathery.

172

1

Fig. 72

First Coat

Mix apple green. Use #8 brush. Trace the design onto onionskin paper and transfer to china with graphite. If a background is desired, it must be applied and fired first before the design is traced on. With green spray, apply apple-green background with ½-inch brush and fire. Trace in the basic spray only.

STEP 2 —With the side of #8 brush, using a loose, broken stroke, put in spray with apple green.

STEP 3 — With a broken stroke, add fronds with apple green.

Metallic trim may be added following the special instructions in Chapter 3. Dry and fire.

Second Coat

Retrace design on china. Mix dark-green, brown-green. Use #8 brush.

STEP 4 — With the side of a well spread brush, stroke in dark green over apple green (this cannot be done with a OO pointer).

STEP 5 — Add small wide strokes at the base of each frond with brown-green.

Add second application of metallic trim, if desired, following special instructions. Dry and fire.

174

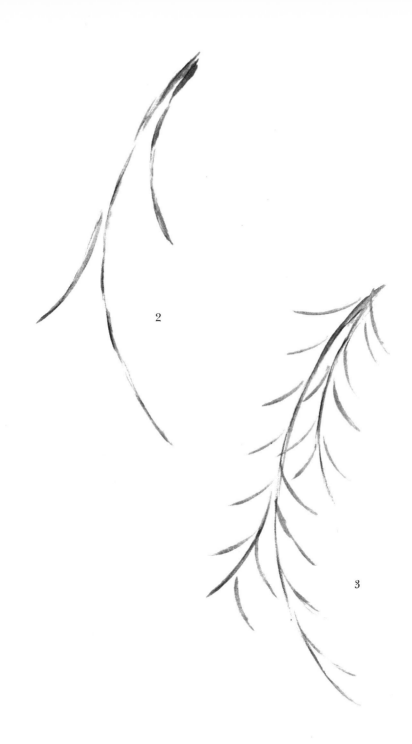

Fig. 73

4

5

Fig. 74

6

Fig. 75

LEAF VARIATION FOR FERN DESIGN

First Coat

STEP 6 — Trace in basic design.
STEP 7 — With well spread #8 brush, using S stroke, paint in leaves
with light shade of color desired. When painting leaves, stroke
each leaf away from the stem. Leaves should be placed on alternate
side of the stems.

Apply metallic trim, if desired, following the special instructions
in Chapter 3. Dry and fire.

Second Coat

STEP 8 — With #8 brush, put a small comma stroke at base of each
leaf with a darker shade of the original color. Stroke in stems.

Apply metallic trim following the special instructions in Chapter
3. Dry and fire.

Color Variation

First coat	Light blue
Second coat	Dark blue
	Shadow with blue-gray

7

8

Fig. 76

19

Special-Occasion Pieces

(FIGURES 77-80)

Figure 77

STEP 1 — This is the design for a wedding plate. Refer to chapters on baby pink rose and forget-me-not for specific brush instructions. Use #4 brush on forget-me-not and #8 brush for rose. Trace design onto onionskin and apply to china with graphite paper. Apply this first coat on flowers. Add printing, if desired, with OO pointer. Outline bells and ribbon with metallic trim (Roman gold or paste white gold). Liquid trim will not go over wax lines.

First firing. No background is needed.

Second Coat

Finish flowers. Add second coat of trim. Fire.

Third Coat

Trace in and paint shadows. Intensify flowers where needed. Touch up trim if needed. Fire.

180

Fig. 77

Figure 78

STEP 2 — This is the design for a small, personalized jewelry box. Specific instructions for applying buttercups begin in Step 4. It is attractive, particularly for youngsters, to add a bee or ladybug to the design.

For small articles such as powder boxes, you may trace directly from this design. Or, you may trace from the color plate to make pins or brooches. Remember that the color plate has been reduced one third in size.

STEP 3 — This design is for a personalized baby cup. You may apply it as shown in the color plate, adding the name on one side and the birth date to the other side with one spray of bluebells. Bluebell instruction begins in Step 13.

You may trace from this design which is the correct size or you may trace any part of the design from the color plate to make pins, earrings or ring boxes.

Baby prints

Applying a baby's footprint to an ashtray or tile can be easily done. Cover his foot with a thin coat of black to which a drop of anise oil has been added with the regular medium. Press the foot firmly against the center of the china. Liquid palladium trim in attractive with the baby's footprint. Dry and fire.

The baby's hand may also be done in the same manner. However, unless the baby is soundly asleep, he will tend to curl his hand into a fist. Wash the paint off the baby with coap and water immediately.

2

3

Fig. 78

Buttercups

Trace design onto onionskin and apply to china with graphite paper. Mix pale yellow, apple green. Use #4 brush.

Step 4 — Fill all flower petals with pale yellow.
Step 5 — Paint bee with pale yellow.
Step 6 — Fill centers and feather in leaves with apple green.

Backgrounding

Use ½-inch brush. Cover with pale yellow, edge with apple green. Blend and pad. Add metallic trim. Dry and fire.

Second Coat

Retrace design on to china.
Mix lemon yellow, yellow-brown, brown-green, yellow-red, black.

Step 7 — With #4 brush, using C stroke, shade all petals with lemon yellow. Keep heavy side of brush toward base of petal.
Step 8 — With #4 brush, using corner stroke, outline around central flower with yellow-brown.
Step 9 — Using OO pointer, make short broken strokes to mark petal divisions, with yellow-brown.
Step 10 — Using #4 brush, shade one dot in center of each flower and fill bud calyx with brown-green. Feather in all leaves with brown-green.
Step 11 — With OO pointer, make circle of dots around center of each flower with yellow-red.
Step 12 — Using OO pointer, outline bee and mark detail with black.

Second Background

Apply yellow-red over pale yellow, around main clump as shown. Darken apple green if needed. Blend and pad. Add metallic trim following previous instructions. Dry and fire.

184

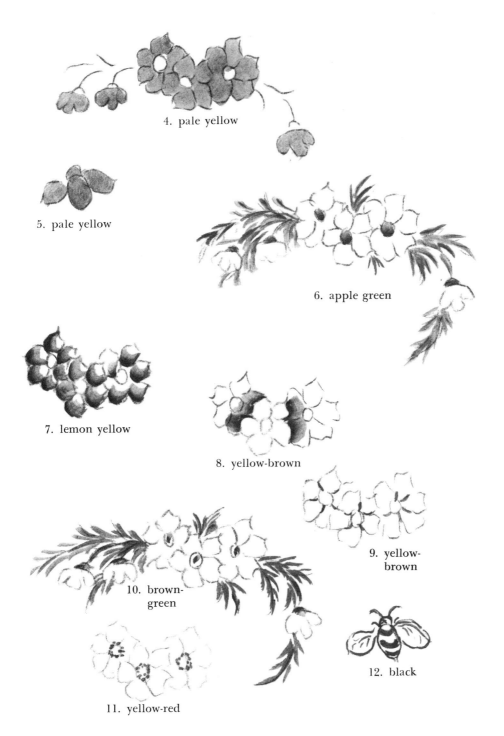

4. pale yellow

5. pale yellow

6. apple green

7. lemon yellow

8. yellow-brown

9. yellow-
brown

10. brown-
green

11. yellow-red

12. black

Fig. 79

Baby Cup

Trace on leaf spray of bluebells only for first coat (butterfly and flower will be added later). Mix lemon yellow, blue-green, baby blue. Use #4 brush.

STEP 13 — Coat leaves with lemon yellow.
STEP 14 — Put small comma stroke on base of each leaf with blue-green.

Background and First Firing

With ½-inch brush, coat upper half of the cup with pale yellow. Be sure to coat area where butterfly will appear. Coat lower half of cup with baby blue. Blend and pad. Add metallic trim. Dry and fire.

Second Coat

Trace in design completely. Mix brown-green, baby blue, black.

STEP 15 — With #8 brush, using broken S stroke, shade leaves with brown-green. Feather in stems of bluebells with brown-green.
STEP 16 — With #4 brush, using small C stroke, stroke in bluebells, with baby blue. Make them larger at the bottom and smaller at the top.
STEP 17 — Using OO pointer, line in butterfly detail with black. With #8 brush, outline tip edges of wings with black.

Second Background

Apply yellow-red accent over pale yellow. Blend, do not pad. With OO pointer, add lettering with liquid metallic trim over the previously fired background. You may letter with color, if desired. Dry and fire.

186

13. lemon yellow

14. blue-green

15. brown-green

16. baby blue

17. black

Fig. 80

20

Forget-Me-Not Design

(Color Plate XVII; Figures 81-85)

a — Topmost complete flowers
b — Incomplete flowers. Note that
some petals are underneath
(a) flowers
c — Leaves beneath flowers
d — Isolated flowers
e — Isolated leaves
f — Buds
g — Shadows

Figures 81, 82

STEPS 1, 2 — Trace from these designs for small plates, switch plates, door knobs, jewelry boxes or bonbon dishes. When doing a large coffee or tea pot, scatter the small designs, three on the front and three on the back.

Keep paint thin and light on the flowers. Shade flowers properly and do not cover all of petals with paint. Keep flowers full and overlapped.

188

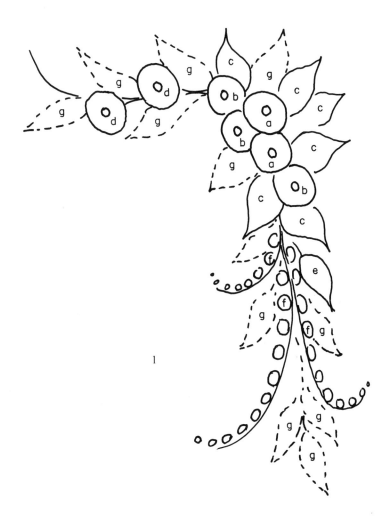

l

Fig. 81

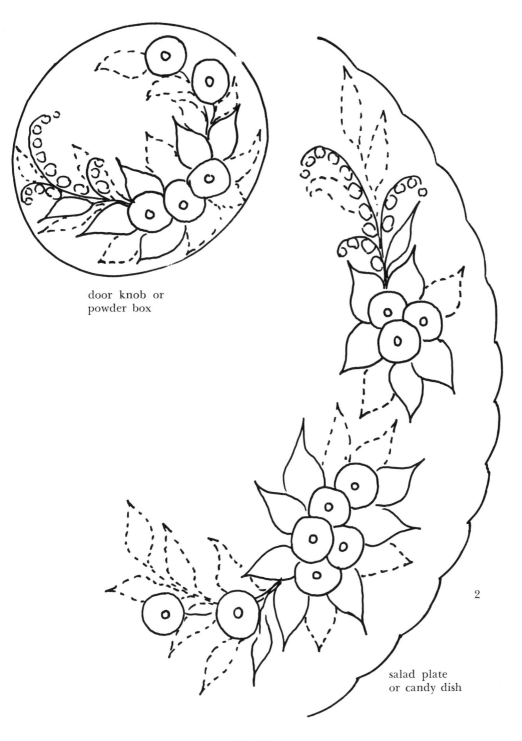

door knob or
powder box

2

salad plate
or candy dish

Fig. 82

First Coat

Trace the design from the text onto onionskin paper and transfer to china with graphite paper. Do not trace in shadows or stems on china for the first coat.

Mix lemon yellow, apple green, baby blue.

STEP 3 — With OO pointer, fill centers of all flowers with lemon yellow.

STEP 4 — With #4 brush, paint around centers with baby blue. Keep paint very thin on the brush. Cover whole blossom.

STEP 5 — With #8 brush, using comma stroke, shade tips of lower leaves with lemon yellow.

STEP 6 — With #8 brush, using corner stroke, shade on base of top leaves with lemon yellow.

STEP 7 — With #8 brush, using S stroke, shade tips of top leaves with apple green. Turn plate as you stroke.

STEP 8 —With #8 brush, using comma stroke, paint base of lower leaves with apple green. Blend green into yellow if necessary so there is no harsh line between the colors.

Background and First Firing

Mix pale yellow and baby blue.

With ½-inch brush, or #10 brush, stroke over X areas with light yellow. Paint center area with light yellow. Paint remainder of area with baby blue as in the color plate.

Be sure to keep baby blue on *outer edge* of flat piece and on the *base* of upright pieces. Blend and pad. Dry and fire first coat.

192

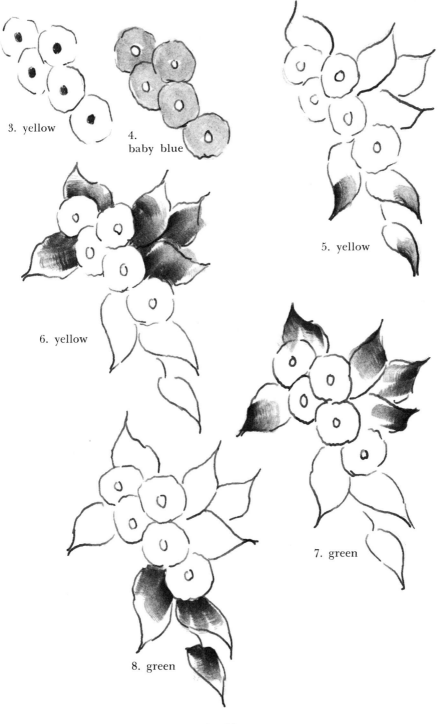

3. yellow

4.
baby blue

5. yellow

6. yellow

7. green

8. green

Fig. 83

Second Coat

Mix baby blue, yellow-red, any blue gray such as silver, brown-green and Persian blue. Retrace design on china. Do not trace in shadows.

STEPS 9, 10 — Using OO pointer, sketch in petals for the two complete flowers with baby blue. Keep petals round. Draw petals on incomplete flowers. Notice that where blossoms overlap, petals are incomplete.

STEP 11 — With #4 brush, using C stroke, shade left side of each petal on the two complete flowers with Persian blue. *Do not* rotate piece. Shade paint carefully on the brush, heavy on the left to almost nothing on the right.

STEP 12 — With #4 brush, using C stroke, shade only complete petals of the other flowers in the same manner with Persian blue.

STEP 13 — With OO pointer, make a dotted semicircle around right side of flower centers with Persian blue.

STEP 14 — With OO pointer, put dot on right side of each center with yellow-red.

STEP 15 — Mix one-half brown-green and one-half blue-gray. With #8 brush, using broken strokes, shade base of all leaves. Keep heavy side of the brush toward blossom and rotate plate as you stroke. Cut in closely between petals.

STEP 16 — With #8 brush, using broken comma stroke, paint edge of leaf tips (leaf tips should point down). When painting lower tips, cut in from the edges (to give effect of slightly upturned leaves.

STEP 17 — With #8 brush, outline around the design over the light yellow background with yellow-red. Keep heavy side of the brush toward flower centers.

STEP 18 — With the side of #8 brush well spread, feather in the already traced stems with green-gray mixture.

STEP 19 — With #4 brush, using small uneven C strokes toward tips of spray, shade with Persian blue.

(continued on page 196)

194

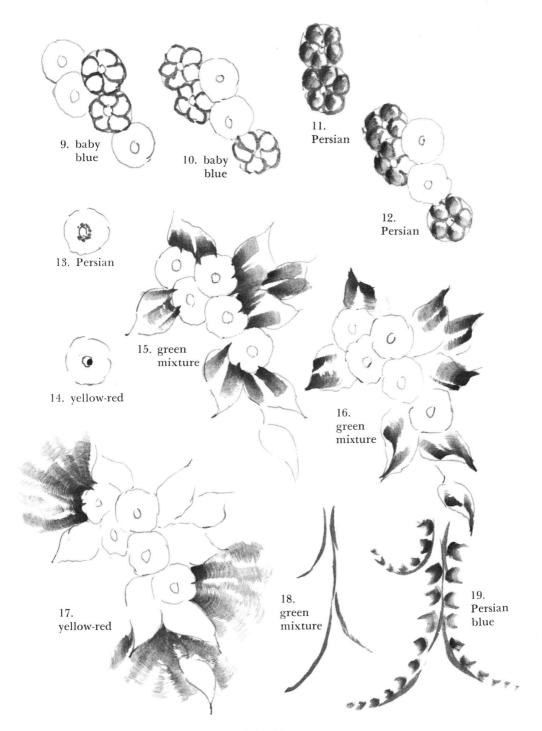

9. baby
   blue

10. baby
    blue

11.
Persian

12.
Persian

13. Persian

14. yellow-red

15. green
    mixture

16.
green
mixture

17.
yellow-red

18.
green
mixture

19.
Persian
blue

Fig. 84

Second Background (Optional)

Mix pale yellow and baby blue. Apply over first background. Blend, avoid padding if possible. Gold or other metallic trim may be added. Dry and fire.

Third Coat

Mix Persian blue (or any blue darker than baby blue), .yellow red, blue-gray.

STEP 20 — With #4 brush, using broken stroke, outline top flower with Persian blue.

STEP 21 — With #4 brush, outline where any flower is under another. Use Persian blue.

STEP 22 — With OO pointer, darken centers with yellow red.

STEP 23 — Trace in shadows from onionskin paper using graphite paper for transfer. With #4 brush, using long S stroke, paint with blue-gray. Rotate piece as you paint.

Apply second coat of gold or other metallic trim, if desired, following the special instructions. Dry and fire third coat.

Color Variation

First coat	Any soft pink.
Background	Pale pink, baby blue, pale yellow.
Second coat	Persian or baby blue.
Buds	Pale pink.
Second background	Purple over blue.
Shadows	Gray with a little pink added.

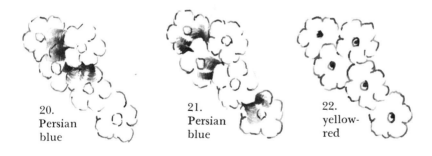

20.
Persian
blue

21.
Persian
blue

22.
yellow-
red

23.
shadow mixture

Fig. 85

21

Gold Rose Design

(Figures 86-88)

Figure 86

Step 1 — This is the master tracing for a gold rose as shown in Color
Plate XIX. If a background is desired, pad complete plate with
pale yellow or any brown-toned ivory. Fire. Use unfluxed gold
over a fired background. If no background has been applied,
use fluxed Roman gold. Use a new pat of gold, this avoids
contamination.

First Coat

Trace in the double lined edge of the main design from Step 1.
Apply gold within this area. Keep gold in thin consistency. Add gold
trim on edge of plate. Fire.

Second Coat

Do not trace in design. Fill in second coat of gold over first, keeping gold thin. Add trim on edge. Fire. Polish gold to the highest gloss
possible.

198

Fig. 86

Third Coat

STEP 2 — Trace in rose detail but not shadows.

Mix red-brown, or blood red and brown in equal ratios. Any color used should be test fired over gold and polished, to be sure it will not rub off. This is because the amount of flux included in colors will vary with each manufacturer.

With #8 brush, shade in all rose markings with red-brown. See color plate and refer to Rose chapter, if necessary, for brush strokes. Dry and fire.

STEP 3 — Trace in shadows from Step 1. Intensify markings on rose with red-brown if needed. With loose strokes add shadows with red-brown. Dry and fire.

201

2

Fig. 87

3

Fig. 88

22

Baby Black Roses—Monochrome Design

(FIGURES 89-93)

Monochrome is painting done in a single color. It sometimes makes a more dramatic effect than a combination of colors. Monochrome is particularly attractive on dinnerware, and black is commonly used in these cases. Gray with a little dark blue mixed into it makes a nice variation, and also green with a bit of dark blue added in.

Candlesticks in monochrome, matching the dinnerware, help make a pretty table setting, as do also salt and peppers. Side dishes, bonbon plates and tiered tidbit trays are all effectively painted in monochrome.

For the coffee table, try a cigarette and lighter set with ashtrays to match painted in black and personalized with names, if desired. A lighter motif would be a complete dresserware set done in pink monochrome.

204

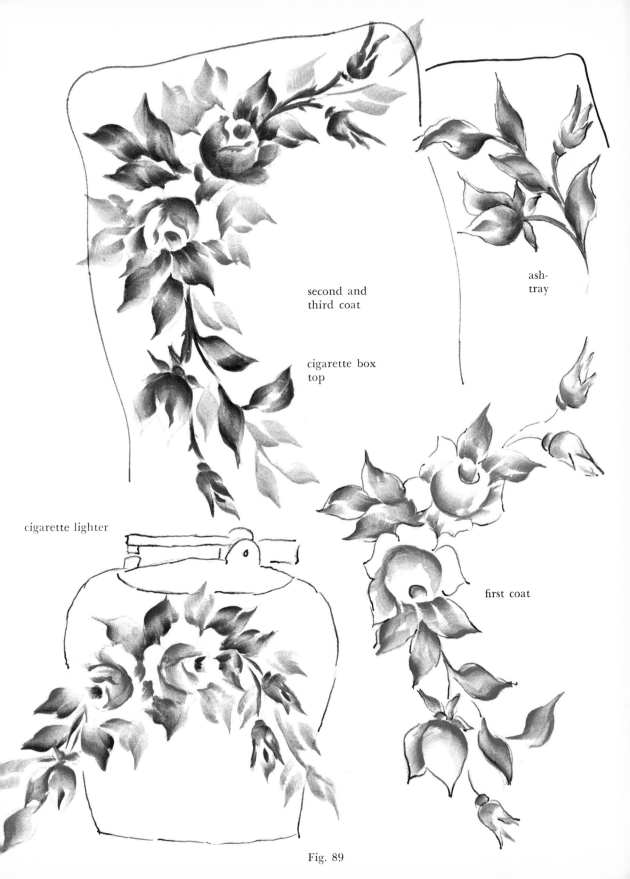

second and
third coat

ash-
tray

cigarette box
top

cigarette lighter

first coat

Fig. 89

Figure 90

a — Completely outlined flower
b — Incomplete flower
c — Leaves underneath flower
d — Leaves underneath leaves
e — Partially open flower
f — Buds
g — Isolated leaves attached to stems
h — Shadows

Trace from this design to apply on the top of cigarette box. As shown in Figure 89, designs may be used on ash trays, cigarette lighters, small vases, or dinnerware. Keep the color light. Shade the brush properly with paint and use your finger to lift excess paint.

Backgrounding

Backgrounding in monochrome is optional. If it is desired, apply it first, before you apply the design. The china piece will require four firings.

FIRST — Cover lightly with monochrome color. Pad. Fire.
SECOND — Trace the design over the fired background. Paint full design in the same color. Fire.
THIRD — Apply second coat to design. Fire. Add shadows. Fire.

Fig. 90

First Coat

Use #8 brush exclusively when painting the design in this text. For smaller roses, use a #4 brush. Trace the text design onto onionskin paper and transfer to china piece with graphite paper. Do not add shadows or stems on the first coat. Mix black. Paint should be applied very thinly but with proper shading.

STEP 1 — Using C stroke, shade left side of flower bowl.

STEP 2 — Using broken comma stroke, outline right side of bowl.

STEP 3 — Turn plate and put small C stroke in center.

STEP 4 — Using broken stroke, outline where flowers overlap. Keep heavy side of the brush toward completely outlined flower.

STEP 5 — Using broken stroke, shade base of leaves. Keep heavy side of brush toward flower.

STEP 6 — Turn piece so leaf tip points down. Put broken comma stroke on tips of all leaves.

STEP 7 — Turn piece so tip of partially opened flower is to your right. Put small C stroke in bowl of calyx.

STEP 8 — With small S strokes, complete balance of calyx. Turn china as you stroke.

STEP 9 — Using C stroke shade left side of bowl.

STEP 10 — Using broken comma stroke, shade lower half of petal on partial flower.

STEP 11 — Turn piece so tip of partial flower is toward you. Using comma stroke, tip partial flower bowl and petal.

STEP 12 — Turn piece so bud points to your right. Using small C put in base of calyx.

STEP 13 — Using large C, put in balance of calyx.

STEP 14 — Turn piece so bud tip is down. Using long S, put in tips of bud very lightly.

STEP 15 — Using S stroke, paint isolated leaves.

First Firing

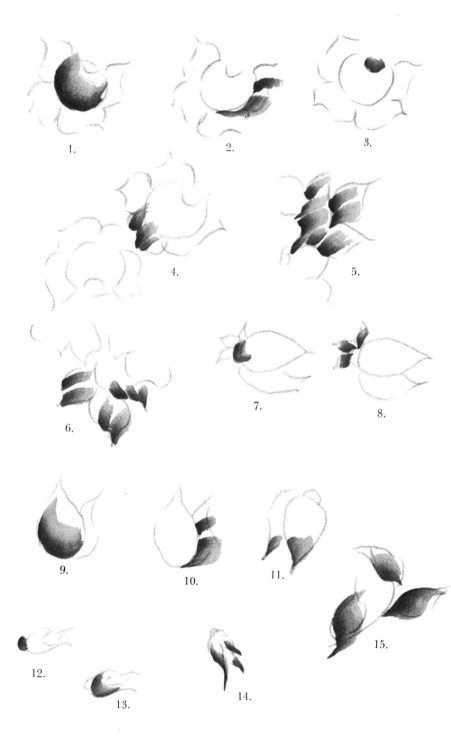

1.

2.

3.

4.

5.

6.

7.

8.

9.

10.

11.

12.

13.

14.

15.

Fig. 91

Second Coat

Retrace design on piece. Do not trace on shadows.

STEP 16 — Using C stroke, darken bowl slightly.

STEP 17 — Using broken comma stroke, outline right side of bowl.

STEP 18 — Using left corner of brush, put three little strokes deep in center.

STEP 19 — Put two long S strokes on each side of center flower, to give petal effects.

STEP 20 — Make small comma strokes to separate all petals.

STEP 21 — Darken slightly where flowers overlap.

STEP 22 — Intensify leaves as desired.

STEP 23 — Using small comma stroke, put center in each leaf.

STEP 24 — Darken partial flower where desired.

STEP 25 — Turn piece so tip of partial flower is down. Make one short comma stroke on tip to give petal effect.

STEP 26 — Intensify first coat on buds.

STEP 27 — Make long S stroke through center to complete bud.

STEP 28 — Darken isolated leaves.

STEP 29 — Using edge of brush and a broken stroke, paint in all stems and add thorns.

Add first coat of metallic trim, palladium preferably, with black roses.

Second Firing

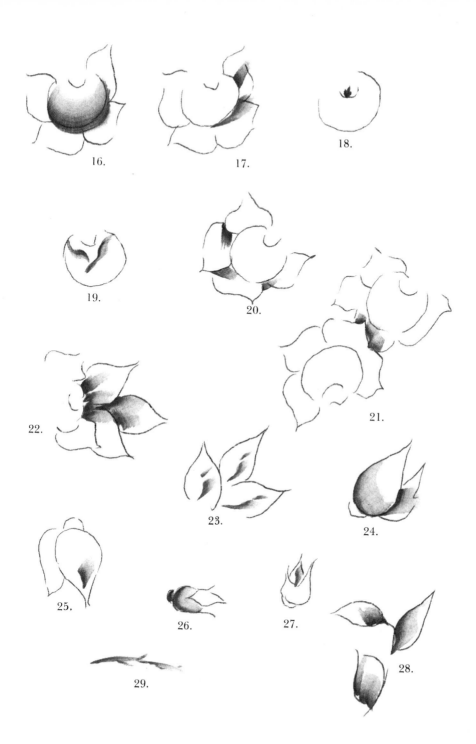

16.

17.

18.

19.

20.

21.

22.

23.

24.

25.

26.

27.

28.

29.

Fig. 92

Third Coat

Trace in dotted shadows from onionskin using graphite paper.

STEP 30 — Feather in shadow stems.
STEP 31 — Using broken S, put in isolated shadow leaves lightly.
STEP 32 — Lightly outline around flowers where shadow leaves are located.
STEP 33 — Turn piece so leaf tips point down. With a comma stroke, tip shadow leaves lightly.

Add final metallic trim and fire.

30.

31.

32.

33.

Fig. 93

23

Firing

The china must be fired in the kiln between each coat of color. Local schools, recreation centers or hobby shops are a few of the places where you may get your firing done. When transporting pieces to be fired, be sure to dry them well and wrap in tissue or wax paper.

In the firing process, the glaze of the china softens and absorbs the china colors. The paint will not come off if properly fired. However, gold and the other metallic finishes adhere to the glazed surface and after many years of use, will wear off.

When you are ready to buy your own kiln, remember that a large kiln will fire all your ware but will take much more electricity and will require a much longer time to reach the desired heat. A smaller kiln will fire all but the largest pieces and does not require special house wiring. It can be plugged into any household outlet provided the full circuit is made available to it. Kilns usually come with complete instruction books.

A kiln to which you may add additional rings to obtain extra height is desirable and enables you to heat only the area needed.

You will also need:

- Clay stilts to separate pieces when stacking them.
- Pyrometric cones, which are used as a heat signal. They bend by melting as the desired temperature is reached. (Cones are available in two sizes.)

- Additional shelves, posts, and stacking racks are optional.
- A sturdy stand, preferably metal, on which to place the kiln.

The first rule to remember is that your kiln must be clean and dry. A protective coat of kiln wash on the bottom and sides of the kiln is advisable when using kiln for the first time. Be careful not to get any of the wash on the wire elements if they are exposed.

During the firing process, kiln dust rises with the heat, and if it settles on the china while the glaze is soft, the colors on the china pieces will be marred. Occasionally, the kiln should be thoroughly cleaned with a soft brush or dry cloth. (The vacuum cleaner brush attachment serves well for this.)

Before stacking the kiln, be sure your china ware is clean and dry. Remove all finger marks and paint smudges from the bottom and gently wipe off any dust with a soft silk cloth.

Your china pieces must be stacked so they do not touch. As the glaze softens, they will stick together if they are touching. The pieces also must have space around them so the hot air can circulate freely on all sides. You should allow at least $\frac{1}{4}$- to $\frac{1}{2}$-inch between the pieces, staying one full inch below the top of the kiln. All but very small pieces should be stilted.

Plates may sit on the floor of the kiln if there is no area on the bottom of the plate which will trap air. Plates, saucers, and trays may be stacked in a pile, preferably not more than three or four in a stack, if you place stilts between each layer so the pieces are separated.

Cups, bowls and similar curved pieces must be stilted to prevent trapping any air which will cause breakage.

Any piece of china can be fired in any position *if* it is stilted, has sufficient space around it to allow for expansion, and is not touching any other piece. It must also retain its proper balance during the entire firing process.

Place the cone inside your kiln in an upright position where it may be easily seen through the peep hole. Cones may be placed in cone holders or propped against a large piece of broken stilt, or set in clay. Make sure clay is dry before starting to fire. Otherwise, it will explode in the firing process.

If there is any doubt about the kiln being perfectly dry, warm the kiln for a few minutes.

When starting to fire, leave the lid ajar or slide it back 2 inches for the first thirty or forty-five minutes to allow the oil to burn off. You will notice that your china painting will turn dark at first and then back to natural color. During this time there will be an odor from the oil that is burning off.

Slide the lid carefully back into place. Wait fifteen to forty-five minutes, depending on the size of the chamber, and check through the peep hole to see if the cone has started to bend.

Check cone each ten minutes, for the next half hour until the cone bends. When cone bends, turn off the kiln switch or pull the plug. Leave the kiln closed and allow it to cool for six to eight hours. Open cautiously. If your kiln has a control switch follow directions of the manufacturer.

Fire the china between 1300 and 1400 degrees. An 018 cone ordinarily will fire all colors if it is allowed to bend well over. If you use an 016 or 017 cone, turn off the kiln as soon as cone begins to bend. Some china requires more heat in order to obtain a good glaze.

If the china is rough when removed from the kiln, try rubbing with damp gold polishing sand. This roughness is often caused by kiln dust partially fired in. If you are particularly bothered by kiln dust, stack your plates bottom side up and the dust will not adhere as readily.

If you find pinpoints of dark color, they may be snapped off with a pointed piece of broken china. Place point at one side of spot and press slowly into the spot.

The reds are problem colors in firing. Most of the other colors will fire without much variation. However, yellow-red will disappear and iron red will turn brown in too hot a kiln.

When firing a piece which is predominantly red, keep it at the bottom of the kiln, or in the center if it is a tall slender piece. Use an 018 cone and turn the kiln off as soon as the cone begins to bend. Purples and rubies require a hot fire, so when you are doing a predominantly purple piece, fire at 016 or let the 018 cone go over and melt down.

One per cent of your ware will crack in the firing process, usually due to imperfections in the china. Breakage usually occurs during the preheating when your lid is open. If this happens, close the lid and unplug the kiln. Cool and remove the broken pieces. Repack the kiln and begin again. Handle partially fired china carefully. Many times the color is like a dust on the surface and your finger will lift it.

24

Tips on Designing

Composing original designs is a challenge. When working up a new pattern, remember to keep it simple. Avoid giving a heavy or overdecorated look. On small pieces of china ware, put a dainty design which will not appear crowded. Reserve the larger, flowered designs for the bigger pieces.

Generally, it is a good rule not to cover more than one third of the china with the design. Covering less rather than more is preferable.

Create a central point of interest which will catch the eye. Surrounding this focal point should be a compact, tight design, not a scattered or spidery looking pattern. For example, one main flower on a cup, surrounded by leaves and two buds, makes a good but simple design. A light rose flanked by two darker roses on either side, with leaves added in small groups, will give an artistic effect. One full bloom flower, also with grouped leaves, centered between a partial flower and a bud is a compact pattern.

Applying a touch of bright yellow or yellow-red in the background behind a flower or bird's head will add a sunshine effect which helps to emphasize the interest point of the design.

Begin your design by sketching the "C" curve. Pattern your flowers along this general outline, putting the main portion of the design in the middle. Add graceful tag ends to your "C" until it becomes an "S" and use this figure as your basic guide step. Vary it in size or shape to suit the particular piece of china. Maintain flowing lines and keep to the basic outline of the china.

An interesting effect can be had by putting small flowers on large pieces. Tea sets, tall water jugs and pitchers can be nicely decorated with little forget-me-nots, baby roses or violets.

Try scattering groups of these smaller flowers. Put three or five groups on a side, being careful not to overdo. Each group should still follow the basic rules of simplicity and flowing lines.

Keep the number of flowers and leaves uneven, one, three, or five. When using a tree branch in the design, give it three or five points.

You may effectively combine two varieties of flowers, baby roses and forget-me-nots, for example, but never more than two. These combinations are very nice for dresser sets. Use the combined design on the lamp, tray and other larger pieces and the plain forget-me-nots on the ring tree, pin tray and the smaller articles. Remember to make a note of your design when the china is planned as a gift, so that your next gift to the same person will blend, particularly in the case of dresser sets.

Designing Dinnerware

When designing dinnerware, keep your pattern on the outer edge. Never put a different flower on each place setting. The overall effect would be confusing. Designs which completely encircle dinnerware must be kept very simple.

One large design at the top of a dinner plate with two smaller side designs is effective. On the salad plate, use just the large design. On the bread and butter plate, put that portion of the design which is on the left side of the dinner plate. On the saucer apply the right portion of the design and repeat the large design on the cup. As long as your design is toward the outer edge of the plate, it still shows when the food is on the dish. One spray of flowers across the top of each plate makes a lovely design.

Designing for Wall Pieces

When doing wall plates or plaques, you may cover more than one third of the piece. Do not crowd the design and remember the rule of uneven numbers. The iridescent effect of china paints is unique and china painted plates for walls or ornamental knickknacks, make handsome decorations for any room.

Keep your dark colors and the bulk of your design at the base of upright pieces. Follow the contour of the china with the design. If there is a good place for gold trim at the base, it will steady the design. Cups, vases, and lamps look well with a trim at the base, for example. Darkest colors in the background should be on the outer edge of a plate.

Great depth of color should be reserved for the large vases, wall plates, lamps and accent pieces created for a special effect.

25

Common Problems in China Painting

The most common and major problem in china painting is loading the brush with too much paint and consequently, applying the paint too heavily on the china. Color should always be applied in thin coats which appear transparent. This is sometimes referred to as applying a thin wash. Here are some other common problems and their solutions.

If the brush splits while in use and the hairs separate:

Clean the brush in turpentine, fill it with oil and condition it by pulling it in a waving motion down the palette.

To prevent future splitting, keep more oil in the brush. Keep the hairs straight. Never scrub with the brush and always apply paint to the brush with a "C" stroke motion.

If the quill of the brush splits when being put on the stick:

Secure it with band of adhesive tape.

To prevent this, soak the quill end of the brush in water before putting it on the stick.

If the brush goes limp, and bends over while painting:

Fill the brush with oil, flatten it between your fingers and then store it for several days in a glass or jar, brush side up.

To prevent this, never wash brushes in soap and water and never leave them sitting in turpentine.

If the brush hairs fall out:

The wire may be loose. Tighten it with pliers. If the brush is a ferrule type, store it for several days, brush side up, to allow the glue to harden.

To prevent this in the case of a ferrule brush, do not leave brushes in turpentine, as this softens the glue.

If brush goes into a point while painting:

Continuously flatten the brush and fan out the hairs while you are painting.

To prevent this, always flatten the brush between your fingers before storing.

If brush hairs or dust are stuck to the wet paint on unfired china:

Remove with the point of a wax china marker.

To prevent, take care not to wear fuzzy clothing, or if the brush is shedding hairs, store it until the glue hardens, or discard it.

If your background is muddy or discolored:

If painting is still wet on the background, remove the muddy area and redo it.

To prevent, backgrounding pad must be clean, the brush clean, the oil clean and the colors clear.

If there are cloth marks on the background after padding:

Redo the background painting, while it is still wet, with a pure silk pad.

To prevent, never use any cloth to made pads except one hundred percent pure silk.

If the background is full of bubbles after padding:

Lay it aside and pad again.

To prevent, use less oil. Mix the oil on the brush well into the color.

If the background dries too quickly before you have time to blend colors:

Remove and start again.

To prevent, add a few drops of lavender oil or add a drop of clove oil to your medium.

If oil seeps from one color to another:

If the painting is still wet, dab it firmly with your finger until the oil line disappears. Do not fire if there is an oil line. If dry, begin again.

To prevent, mix color well into the brush so there is no loose oil on the brush. Take care not to use too much oil in the brush.

If the oil is dirty:

Pour off the clear oil on the top. Wipe out the jar and return the clean oil to jar.

To prevent, periodically wipe out the old paint which will settle on the bottom of the jar. The clear oil on the top is still usable.

If there are purple smudges after firing:

This is caused by gold. Use the gold eraser and take more care when applying gold.

If the gold flakes after firing:

Rub the gold with emory paper or a mild abrasive and apply again.

To prevent, apply gold of thinner consistency over clean china. Flaking is usually caused by oil smudges underneath the gold or by the gold having been applied too heavily.

223

If the color chips after firing:

Rub the china with emory paper and patch the color if possible.

To prevent, do not apply paint too heavily. Use more oil and apply thin coats of paint.

If spots or holes appear in the paint on unfired china:

If they are too noticeable, do not fire. Repaint the china. Splattered turpentine has caused this.

To prevent, remove china that is ready to be fired from your painting table immediately.

If colors fire very glossy:

Do not rework the old paint over and over with turpentine or oil. Loosen once or twice and then discard. You may be using too much oil.

If colors fade in firing:

Repeat painting with the same colors and fire again.

To prevent, use less oil on the brush but keep paint smooth and thin.

If ridges of color appear where the brush has shaded:

Remove the paint and redo.

To prevent, apply less paint toward the edges. Keep color smooth.

If tiny specks of paint appear on a piece after firing:

Snap off specks of paint with a pointed piece of broken china by placing the point at side of spot and pressing hard.

To prevent, do not apply paint too heavily. These specks are kiln specks. If paint has been applied too heavily on any china in the kiln, it will splatter in the firing and often stick to another piece next to it. Sometimes, it will adhere to the side of the kiln and drop onto a piece of china fired later. Be careful when lettering your name on the back of the china. Often, the letters are too heavily applied.

If paint is grainy when applying:

More thorough mixing on the palette is needed. Use the flat edge of the knife and a circular motion.

To prevent, use a drop of fat oil or a small amount of flux, while mixing. Remember that fat oil and flux adds gloss to your paints.

If the china feels grainy when removed from the kiln:

Rub over with a mild cleaning abrasive or with emory cloth. Remember that emory can scratch.

To prevent, clean kiln dust out of kiln with brush attachment of the vacuum cleaner. Brush top of kiln frequently.

26

Dry Dusting and Enamels

Dry Dusting

Dry dusting is used to produce a very deep color which is particularly effective at the base of a lamp or vase. You will need a fine-mesh screen, a new soft brush, and a large piece of paper.

The surface which is to be dry dusted must have at least one coat of background fired on it before dusting.

Coat the surface area with oil and pad with a silk pad which has a piece of lamb's wool inside. Remove most of the oil with the pad and allow the remaining oil to set until the area is slightly tacky. Sift dry paint several times through the screen. Dip the brush into the dry paint and brush color over the tacky surface. It is necessary to apply the oil evenly so that the dry paint will be distributed properly.

A piece of lamb's wool may be used in place of the brush.

Brush off excess color.

It is advisable to experiment first with dry dusting, for it takes some practice before you achieve the desired effect.

Enamels

Enamels come in white powder form and should be mixed with special enamel medium. They may be colored with your regular overglaze china colors. Mix them very thickly as they will spread during the firing process.

Enamels give a raised ridge effect. Apply them in a fine line on the edge of a flower to give an interesting relief effect, or put them in small dots in the centers of flowers to make the centers stand out. Any ornamental pieces are attractive with enameling.

It is better not to use enamels on any ware that will be frequently used, it may chip.

Test enamels before applying to your good ware.

27

Mending Broken China

When you are repairing china which has been broken into pieces, fit the parts together and tie them securely with asbestos cord. Scotch tape will help to hold the bits together but since it will fire off, you must use the cord, also.

Mix "Cement to be Fired" with water until it has the consistency of thin cream and, in the case of a complete break, apply it to both sides. If the piece is only cracked, cement need only be applied to one side. After the cement is dry, scrape off any excess and fire the piece at the regular china fire heat. After firing, hold the piece up to the light to see if it is completely cemented. If not, repeat the process.

Although the cement will hold the parts together, if the crack or break is very wide it may need to be filled with white enamel. In this case, apply your cement first and allow it to dry. Mix the enamel with water or special enamel medium to a thick, pasty consistency. Fill spaces with the enamel. This enamel may be tinted with china colors to match the surrounding colors. Fire.

If you have a small chip on the edge of the china, rub it with a fine grinding stone and cover it with gold or some other metallic finish. When repairing larger nicks, use special nick-filling powder. This must be mixed with turpentine to a very thick consistency. Be sure to dry the piece thoroughly before firing.

228

Small holes and dark spots may be filled with white enamel. Roll a small bit of enamel between your fingers and shape it into a pointed cone. Press the cone into the hole and break it off even with the surface. Be sure there is no excess enamel left on the surface of the china. In some cases, several fillings will be necessary.

After firing, if you have a raised place on the china from excess enamel, chip it off with a piece of broken china.

Words Used in China Painting

CHINA BLANKS — Glazed, undecorated, vitreous china pieces.

CHINA PAINTING — Painting on glazed ware with overglaze colors.

CONES — Cone-shaped pieces of a clay substance used to measure temperature, and constructed to bend when indicated heat is reached.

CRAZING — Unintentional cracking of the glaze.

FERRULE BRUSH — A brush with a metal band, usually with the hairs glued in.

FIRING — Heating ware in kiln to maturing temperature.

GLAZE — Glassy coating on china.

INTENSITY — Depth of color.

KILN — Oven or furnace.

KILN WASH — Protective coating used inside kiln.

ONIONSKIN — Thin tracing paper.

OVERGLAZE — Low fire glaze put over a harder glaze.

LOADING — Applying paint on brush.

MEDIUM — The oil used for china painting. There is an all-purpose medium, also special mediums for special purposes.

OIL — Common reference to all purpose medium.

OPEN — Refers to paint on china not being dry, can still be worked over with another color.

PAD — Piece of lamb's wool enclosed in a pure silk cloth.

PADDING — Process of gently dabbing on the wet background with the pad to blend colors.

QUILL — Brush with hairs inserted in a quill and bound with wire.

STACKING — Loading the kiln.

SHADE — Refers to paint applied on the brush from dark to light across the full spread of the brush.

STRENGTH — Color depth or intensity.

STILT — Three-pointed clay support used to prop ware in kiln.

TEST — Firing a sample plate to see effect after firing.

TINT — Light coat of paint; also called a thin wash.

TONE — Varied shade of color from light to dark.

TREATMENT — Colors used in painting.

VITREOUS — Hard.

WASH — Thin coat of paint.

Index